Adam's Journey

Adam's Journey

Rare Mitochondrial Disease,
One Family's Search for a Miracle.

Margaret M. McCarthy

PRINCIPIA
MEDIA

Adam's Journey: Rare Mitochondrial Disease, One Family's Search for a Miracle.
© 2012 Margaret McCarthy Jirous
Published by Principia Media, LLC, Grand Rapids, MI
www.principiamedia.com

ISBN-13: 978-1-61485-309-1

Printed in the United States of America

18 17 16 15 14 13 12   7 6 5 4 3 2 1

Cover Design and Interior Layout: Frank Gutbrod

Chapter 1

"Ouch," Joe shouted, as Katie's nails bit into the flesh of his hand, turning it a chalk like color. Leaning down, he kissed her forehead. Joe would gladly trade places with her. The doctor stood yelling "Come on Katie, one more push," as if cheering on a little league player. Suddenly Adam came forth and tears of joy replaced the hours of intense pain that had shrouded Katie's face. Katie wiped a tear from her cheek and said, "Look at him Joe, he's so beautiful." "That he is," Joe replied, as they cradled their beautiful boy and kissed his soft skin.

A thought occurred as Joe picked up the room phone, "I should call home and let your mom know Adam is here. She can tell the kids in the morning." As he punched in the numbers, Katie called out, "Honey I'm sorry about your hand." "Don't worry," Joe replied, "You win the pain prize anyway." The doctor did a quick exam and, finding no apparent problems, left the room leaving the nurse in charge. As she bathed and dressed the baby, Katie and Joe dined on sliced turkey sandwiches and apple juice, in spite of the fact it was almost 2:30 a.m.

A very faded, dark blue vinyl chair, that offered little comfort in its original state, was now pushed and prodded until grudgingly giving way, as if daring Joe to spend what was left of the night on it. Katie was tucked into what had recently been the birthing table, but now, with both an additional piece screwed into the lower end, and sheets and blankets, it had become her bed. Both parents were quiet for a time, as Adam nursed and fell asleep. Joe gently placed him in the see-through bassinet on wheels, and asked Katie as he did so, if the rules on positioning the baby had changed since their last one. Getting no response, he turned and realized Katie was making those little puffing sounds which could only mean she was asleep.

Joe made an effort to get settled on the recliner, but gave up trying to will sleep that just wouldn't come. He began instead to reflect a little on the past. Well, a new baby will do that to you, he reasoned, as he shook his head in amazement that he and Katie had been married almost thirteen years. They had met in the midst of the chaotic circulation department, at The Grand Rapids Press. As he precariously juggled a phone in each hand, a stack of loose papers, a list of paperboy phone numbers, several pencils, and a large mug of coffee, Joe yelled into one of the receivers, "Well wake him up, the papers were supposed to be out an hour ago." Besieged with complaints that districts 10 and 14 were each short 20 and 18 papers respectively, he yelled into the second receiver orders to remedy the situation. Marshaling the paper boys to get excited about delivering papers in two feet of snow or 94 degree heat was what it was all about for him. Keeping them supplied with the necessary papers was critical to that task.

One spring morning, the circulation department collectively dropped its jaw, as Joe showed up in a full Easter bunny costume, even with ears flopping as he walked. He had a carnation for each lady present and a full bouquet for the beautiful girl with dark hair and curls cascading over each shoulder. She too was attached to a phone, only hers was cradled in the spot created when the cheek and shoulder meet. The other hand held a pencil as she furiously wrote out word for word the customer's complaint. Joe didn't have much dating experience to speak of, or basically none, but he could sure see marriage to that girl in his future. That was the day she finally agreed to a date, and just after Christmas, four years later, they were married in a church resplendent with red and white Poinsettias.

They both wanted a large family and have been blessed with five boys and a girl.

The first couple of months following Adam's birth went by quickly. Then one morning right after Christmas, while getting Adam dressed, Katie remarked, "You know Joe, Adam doesn't seem to be growing much. All the previous kids were in larger sleepers by now." Joe responded with all the reassurance he could muster and because he couldn't think of anything else, "Maybe he's just going to be smaller than the other kids."

The concerns of not only his size, but that he wasn't nursing well and taking in enough nourishment, were addressed the following week during Adam's four-month check up. His weight and length were below normal. The doctor labeled him as failure to thrive and suggested doing a feeding evaluation for a couple of days. This would be done as an inpatient service, but the doctor believed it would probably solve the problem.

The lactation consultant concluded Adam was not nursing properly. He was not taking in adequate amounts of milk. Katie commented that he had begun to spit up often and sometimes in fairly large amounts but this was met with minimum concern by the medical staff, who felt it was all related to feeding and would eventually straighten out. They went home with tips on nursing and an order to buy a baby scale, and thus record his weight everyday. Katie would now pump her milk and give it to Adam from a bottle, so every drop could be measured.

About this age babies are introduced to food, but as Katie began giving Adam baby food, she found that most foods made him gag and the spitting up was gradually becoming vomiting. A probable virus or an unresolved problem in learning to eat were the reasons most often given in response to his parent's growing concerns. The doctor did say a swallow study would be scheduled if Adam's eating did not improve soon.

In mid April, following two days of watching Adam vomit off and on and sleep unusually long periods of time, Katie was beside herself with worry. Knowing she couldn't handle once again being told he probably had a virus, she made an appointment with the pediatrician for early the next morning. With the children in bed, Katie snuggled next to Joe on the love seat as he held Adam. With her head on his shoulder and her right hand caressing Adam's cheek, she whispered, "I don't want to spend another night unable to sleep worrying about Adam. That appointment tomorrow is so far away." Feeling his heart beat faster, as the same fear washed over him, Joe said, "See if your mom can stay with the kids, and we'll take him to the emergency room tonight." By the time Katie packed the essentials for Adam, Grandma had arrived, and with a promise to call her as soon as they knew anything, they left for the hospital.

The bright overhead lights revealed a waiting room packed with small children, each accompanied by at least one adult. Katie put a blanket over the sleeping baby, to cover his face, as coughs and sneezes permeated the air. The triage nurse finally called Adam's name, did an assessment of symptoms, and took his temperature. She repeated the current theme that it was most likely the virus going around and they would see the doctor shortly.

When their turn came, they entered a small exam room enclosed by white curtains topped with mesh and attached to tracks in the ceiling. As they waited, Adam vomited covering himself and the floor. The nurse brought towels, a tiny hospital gown, and cleaning supplies. Shortly after, the doctor promptly engaged them in small talk, revealing he had seen numerous cases with the same symptoms that evening.

Completing the routine check of heart, lungs, and ears, he began to palpate various parts of Adam's body. The nurse, having taken a small sample of blood, quickly reported a blood sugar level of 15. Normal blood sugars in a child are the same as an adult ranging from 80-120.

The quiet of the small room was shattered like glass, as the attending doctor forcefully ordered labs, glucose, and "Help in here," all with the word stat attached. Katie whispered frantically to Joe, "What's happening?" Joe just held her tightly, as any thoughts he had, were too frightening to voice. Seemingly out of nowhere, came six or seven doctors and residents, along with a handful of nurses. A large group for a very small room, and as hard as Katie and Joe tried to remain still, they found themselves displaced and pressed against the back curtain of the cubicle.

It was determined the quickest way to get glucose into Adam's system was by a direct injection into the bone marrow. While one team worked on that, someone else tried to draw enough blood for labs. After numerous pokes produced no blood from his little veins, a central line was inserted. That meant using a needle to place a tube into a vein, and thread it up to the chest portion of the large vein or vena cava. The IV tubing left in place would ensure accessibility to the venous system.

On and on it went for the next several hours. Tests were done and samples taken. One of the many procedures nicked Adam's lung, so a chest tube was inserted. In addition to the frantic confusion around them, Joe and Katie could hear Adam scream uncontrollably, and were powerless to help him. Katie's throat was dry and constricted from sheer fear welling up; it was painful to swallow, if not impossible, and any sobs were now more of a constant gasp for air. Joe retreated inside himself to say a few words of prayer, which always had been a big part of his life, but now a myriad of emotions ran through him, making the words hard to find.

When he finally left Adam's side, the doctor looked at the two tear-streaked faces before him and said, "If you had waited until morning to seek care, Adam would not have made it." Katie and Joe considered this, and knew immediately they had been given a miracle that night. The knot that had grown steadily in Katie's stomach, now threatened to explode. So many questions swirled inside, but the only one they could ask, the only one that mattered was, "Is Adam going to be all right?" The doctor would only confirm that Adam would be admitted to the hospital, and the work of diagnosing his problems would begin.

Chapter 2

They were moved to the Pediatric ICU when the initial testing was completed and the IV lines were in. While waiting for the move, Katie called home to let her mother know what had transpired, saying, "We just don't know when we will be home. Kiss the kids and tell them I will call in the morning." Katie and Joe spent what was left of the night trying, with no success, to make sense of what was happening and scared to death of what might be ahead. Exhausted and weak, Adam slept.

As the sun came up, taking his jacket and a list, Joe left for a quick trip home to pick up toothbrushes, toothpaste, and a couple sets of clean clothes to accommodate the unexpected stay in the hospital.

When Joe returned, a nurse took Katie to the hospital computer room and introduced her to the hospital website called CarePages. Each patient has his own page on which a parent, or if old enough the patient himself, could update information and give results of tests to family and friends. This would become their link to the outside world and could be used for as long as they wanted it, both in the hospital and at home. Katie invited family and friends to log in anytime. Word had spread that Adam was in the hospital, and now anyone interested could log into a computer and get an update.

Katie and Joe also used CarePages to ask for prayers for Adam. Communicating their need for help was crucial, as the doctors had no idea what was wrong with Adam, and once they did would need help with a course of action. Messages of hope and prayer started coming in immediately. During this week, Pope John Paul II died. As Joe gazed through the large windows at the morning bustle of the city sprawled below him, he shared his deep worry with the down to earth pope and asked him to speak directly to Jesus. Over the next few days, other people wrote they too had called on this holy man for help.

The testing, that would become a way of life, had begun. Katie used the hospital computer to update CarePages on a regular basis, often several times a day. She told readers:

> An initial MRI was good, but an x-ray showed the lung has not healed completely, so the chest tube is still needed. We could not hold him in our arms, and asked Jesus once again to hold him for us. He did, because that day Adam became more alert, was awake longer, and produced the most beautiful smile I have ever seen. An NG tube was inserted through his nose into the stomach, through which formula will be given. Lots of blood work has been done, and we are waiting for the results, so much information is coming from the Mayo Clinic. We are also asking for many prayers. The visual for us is a Heaven full of prayers for little Adam, and prayers to cover the doctors as they search for answers. The kids at home need prayers too. They miss mommy and daddy so much. And as much as we miss them, neither of us can leave Adam's side right now. We have missed Jackie's First Reconciliation, in preparation for First Communion, and taking her for pictures prior to her dance recital next month. Family filled in for us on these occasions, and we know the kids will be okay, but they need the boost we felt from so many prayers.

Gazing westward, dark storm clouds ranging from smoky grey to black caught Joe's eye because of their threatening appearance.

They appeared to be racing inland from Lake Michigan. Just then, Joe's thoughts were disrupted as he heard the door open, and he was struck by how the storm clouds in the sky were mirrored in the face of the doctor standing before him.

As he approached, Katie and Joe had a deep sense of foreboding. Soon enough his words gave credence to their feelings. "We are leaning," the doctor explained, "towards a rare metabolic disease, and need to do both a muscle and liver biopsy. A few years ago a baby with Adam's symptoms would have been diagnosed as failure to thrive, or to have a liver disease that did not respond to treatment, and for which a cause could not be found."

Katie entered on CarePages:

So here we are on a journey for the answer to a mystery, but surrounded with so much love from those responding to our words. We are ready to accept God's will for Adam, but it never hurts to ask for a miracle, and ask, and ask, and ask.

As Adam slept, his parents shared mom and dad worries such as Joe's comment that, "Grandma is doing a great job taking care of the kids, but they don't understand why this is happening, and why we can't tell them when we will be home."

The next few days brought visits from an occupational therapist, to deal with the effects of lying on his back for a week, and a speech therapist to evaluate why Adam rejects the bottle. The speech pathologist has knowledge of anatomy and functional aspects of the upper aerodigestive tract consisting of the nose, throat, voice box, windpipe, lungs, and swallowing tube. This extensive knowledge of the underlying medical and behavioral etiologies of swallowing and feeding disorders extends to infants, children, and adults. The tests were now back from the Mayo Clinic and all that was known for sure was that more blood work was needed that would be more specific to the metabolic disorders family.

Katie and Joe tried to keep their son occupied with toys, and other distractions, anything to keep him from wanting to be picked up because the chest tube was still preventing that. Their minds swirled with thoughts of: What is the next test? What will it show? Where are we going?

There was a regular testing of his sugar, gradual increases of formula through the feeding tube, and the occasional try of putting formula on Adam's tongue. Gagging and vomiting immediately ensued. He probably didn't get hungry with the feeding tube in, and yet the doctors don't want to let him wait to get hungry, because of the strong probability of a metabolic disorder. The speech therapist, whose assessment will help form the basis for management and treatment, advised patience because the feeding problem could take some time to resolve. She also thought Adam could go home with a feeding tube, but Katie and Joe were more than a little unsure about their ability to handle anything to that medical extent. The therapist believed Adam cried now when he saw a bottle, because he had figured out the direct relationship between it and his tummy discomfort and pain. Katie responded, "Speaking as a mother, it has been easy to get depressed after a failed feeding attempt. Feeding your baby is a way to comfort and nourish him, and it is so upsetting not to be able to do that."

These ordeals tugged at the fragile emotional strings barely holding them together. As she considered this, Katie realized that uplifting messages on the family's CarePage were also surrounding them. There were prayers coming from those they knew and loved, and also from those they didn't know at all, but who were now included in those they loved.

Finally, the chest tube was removed, and the family was transferred from ICU to the general pediatric floor. A nice large room featured two beige recliners, which easily opened into beds. They were treated to days of rocking Adam and letting him fall asleep in their arms. Their belief also grew that God would be patient with them in their frustration. Adam's siblings could also visit now, and it was so good to have the family together. The visits were brief though, and there was always an incredible loneliness when the children left.

The liver and muscle biopsies were done and the specimens sent out. A day later the neurologist indicated that the Mayo Clinic did a retest on one of the original samples sent to them. When Katie updated CarePages she wrote:

> We were given the best in family and friends, as people brought groceries and meals to our family at home, as well as the frequent treat to Joe and me. It looks like Adam does fit the diagnosis they were leaning toward. Long-chain 3 Hydroxyacyl-Coenzyme A Dehydrogenase Deficiency (LCHAD). It means his body cannot metabolize many fatty acids. This can build up in the tissues, and damage the liver, heart, retina, and muscles, potentially causing more serious complications. The good news is that any tests they did on his heart looked good. The liver shows some damage, but so far no scarring. It is an extremely rare metabolic disease. The pool of research is small and new, and they don't know much about it, or how to proceed. The skin biopsy will tell more, and the liver biopsy will confirm the severity of his disease. There is apparently a broad range, and hopefully he will be on the mild side.

Not much in that information does any parent want to hear. However, after ten days a bright spot appeared, and they were going home with Adam.

Chapter 3

"It feels so good to be settled in again," Katie said, taking a minute to relax on the well-worn, but oh so comfortable, couch. Four year old Jacob was snuggled on her lap and rolling her hair around his finger, while Andy, age six, was cuddled under her left arm. Arranged, by category, on the floor were three piles of toys waiting for Adam to play with-- the bouncing kind, stuffed animals, and those requiring someone to pull the attached string. Joey, age eleven, and Aaron, age ten, are both very organized and have set it up so all Adam had to do was choose. Seven year old Jackie, unable to just stand by, made the choice for Adam. A home care nurse was busy setting up a feeding pump and unpacking all the supplies they would need to accommodate this big change in their lives. Katie and Joe agreed it sounded like there would be plenty of support for them. Gently moving Jacob to the couch, Katie stood up and placed a stethoscope around her neck. Then, turning to the nurse she said, "Two weeks ago I was trying to get my sixth grader through English, and now I am listening for placement of a feeding tube in my baby's tummy."

For now feeding would be through the NG tube but an update on CarePages revealed:

If Adam doesn't show signs of taking the bottle or eating, eventually he may have to have a regular g-tube put in. This is surgery so we don't want that to happen. Adam has had the face tape, which holds the tube in place, changed so often that his little cheek started to bleed. Tape sounds like such a minor problem in comparison to what he has been through, but it really is sore for him, and he screams whenever we have to mess with it. It is not known yet if he will need anything adjusted in his diet while he is on formula alone. He is already on many vitamins and Prevacid for his reflux. We know we have to be very watchful for any illness, as this could set him back very quickly. If we can get him to eat solid foods, he will have a special diet, and we must monitor his blood glucose at home. The mortality rate with this diagnosis is pretty high, but the numbers we have seen are several years old. There does seem to be more information available now to help parents and doctors with the treatment. Adam will need to see a neurologist, an endocrinologist, and the gastroenterologist. So much is uncertain in Adam's future, but we have a whole new appreciation for just being together as a family. We love watching as the other kids play with him, enjoy being with him, and he with them.

Three days later, Joe began CarePages with:

Well, how is everyone doing? Here we are back in the hospital. Adam was very fussy last night and developed a fever. Our pediatrician, not wanting to take any chances, sent us to the emergency room. After presenting with such serious symptoms on our last visit, we were given a card which would allow us to be seen with no waiting on any subsequent trips. So in we went, and even ended up in the same exam room. Poor Adam had to be poked a little more, because they missed a few spots last time. Anyway, it was determined he has the cold virus the rest of the kids have and no infection, so one overnight stay for observation and we were sent home. The doctors have worked out a plan now for when Adam is sick. We should be able to judge a little better when he will need emergency medicine, and when he can be treated by the pediatrician as a regular sick kid. We absolutely hated being back in the hospital after thinking we were home to stay. It was also hard on the kids, who had just settled back into our routine and thought this overnight stuff was finished. We are truly blessed that Adam is okay, and everything else we will just deal with. He is still refusing the bottle, and a nurse comes once a week to change the feeding tube. We're glad we don't have to learn to do that. In a couple of weeks our daughter, Jackie, will make her First Communion, and we will focus on the wonderful blessings surrounding that event. We feel the power of prayer surrounding us every time some small detail falls into place to make our lives a little easier.

In May, Adam had his first follow-up visit with the gastroenterologist. There was enough of Adam's newborn blood left for further testing, and it tested negative for the LCHAD. She cautioned, "There is always the possibility of error, but I just don't think he is LCHAD. The biopsy results are not back," she added, "So we don't have any more information to go on." Adam will stay on the current plan of six vitamins a day and feedings every three hours.

Driving home, Katie considered the possibilities. I'm almost afraid to think it's not LCHAD, after resigning ourselves to it, and finally having a diagnosis. But on the other hand, very few of the other metabolic diseases are worse, so if it is another one, that probably is good news.

So another month went by, and Adam once again saw the neurologist and the gastroenterologist. Testing was done to rule out other metabolic disorders. The liver biopsy did not provide enough of a specimen to test for the fructose metabolic disorder. The GI doctor was researching whether any labs out there could use the skin biopsy samples to test for the fructose disorder. Duke University Hospital, which was working on the skin biopsy, could not. If no one else could, then Adam would need to have an open liver biopsy, which would mean a short hospital stay.

Katie updated CarePages to let her readers know:

At that time they will probably put in the permanent feeding tube. The skin biopsy results should tell us which of the fatty oxidation disorders he has. Adam's biggest problem right now is that he really wants to eat solids. He is finally showing an interest in real food and we can't give him any because the doctors have said no fats or sugars until we know more. That leaves him with green vegetables and he tends to gag on them. He'll nibble a cracker and tries a bite of mashed potatoes. Developmentally we think he is about six to eight weeks behind, but he is sitting up well although showing no signs of crawling. For some reason he hates to be on his tummy, and so gets no practice with rolling or scooting. He is a happy baby and other than his very small size, people who see him are surprised he is sick. The doctors continue to be amazed at how quickly he bounced back from his episode, and how well he looks now. We are focusing our prayers at this time on guidance for the doctors, as they continue to search for a diagnosis. We pray we will get some results back so we can open up a food group to him, and let him eat something. He still weighs only a little over fifteen pounds and has grown about an inch since he left the hospital. Joe and I are now changing Adam's feeding tube weekly on our own. Amazing how the things you think you can never do somehow become possible.

In July, Adam saw the neurologist again. Later in the day Katie wrote to family and friends:

> Just as we feared, the skin biopsy was inconclusive. The doctor said the test results were normal, but that it doesn't rule out mitochondrial disorders. He still thinks Adam has a disorder that may never be identified. We didn't handle that one too well, and our emotions tumbled out in a torrent of tears. The doctor wanted to get a second opinion at the Cleveland Clinic and requested further tests on the skin biopsy samples, by a metabolic specialist at Baylor University in Dallas.

The neurologist somehow made this happen and one month later the results came in from Baylor, and another message from Katie said:

> They were negative for LCHAD, which is so serious because of the potential for damage to other organs. The hereditary fructose intolerance is still a possibility, so we can't give Adam any sugar or fruits and most vegetables. The next step is a fructose challenge test to be done in the hospital ICU. Adam will be given fructose through an IV and monitored closely for any signs of trouble. If the test is negative, then he either has something so rare they can't test for it, or he has had some powerful healing. We vote for that.

As sugar was now off limits, Adam celebrated his first birthday in September with a sugarfree Jell-O mold and one large candle.

Chapter 4

Adam's open liver biopsy was scheduled for December, and the specimen was tested for anything causing elevated liver enzymes. If there were no complications, it should only be a one-night stay in the hospital. The surgeons planned to make a small incision through Adam's abdomen into the stomach and would insert a small tube used when patients cannot take enough food by mouth to maintain their weight. It's called a g-tube and is opened with a small flap on the outside of the abdomen. Tubing was inserted through the flap and the formula was given. The day of the biopsy came and went with no complications. Katie and Joe began learning their way around the new tube and loved the fact that Adam's cheeks would no longer be red from the constant tape.

When the long wait for biopsy results finally ended, the doctors indicated that it could be a disease called mitochondrial complex I deficiency; however the endocrinologist didn't think this was the complete picture, believing there was much more to learn about Adam's condition. He took the time to search for a geneticist and wrote a letter to a doctor in Pittsburgh who specializes in inborn errors of metabolism.

In November of 2006, Katie and Joe took Adam on a road trip to Children's Hospital of Pittsburgh. They went to meet Dr. Gerard Vockley, MD, PhD, division chief, medical genetics, and professor of human genetics and pediatrics. Under his direction many more tests on the tissue samples that had already been taken were done. He would also manage Adam's care and believed his metabolic disorder was even more rare than the doctors in Grand Rapids had suspected, possibly identified only in the last few years. During this visit, Katie and Joe learned a lot more about how many of Adam's symptoms were related. Katie wrote later that day:

> We have been asking for prayers for the doctors involved in Adam's case and we can see the fruits of that in the people we meet in Pittsburgh.

Katie was back at the hospital computer in January, when a bout of low blood sugar and vomiting sent Adam to the hospital:

> IV fluids stabilized him quickly, but the horror of the time in the ER was still on our minds. It took more than an hour for the staff to insert the IV line. Poke after poke was required, until the head of the children's intensive care finally got it in. All of this was too much for us as parents to watch. We prayed for our baby to be safe in our arms, but we kept it together through all the prayers we received. We were able to take Adam home after a day and a half in the hospital. He seems to be fighting a virus, and we are now monitoring his blood sugars at home. They haven't been what they should be, but they haven't been low enough to go back to the ER.

By May, Adam's blood sugar levels had become consistently low, and the doctors put him on round-the-clock feedings. The plan was for him to wear a little backpack all day containing a small feeding pump, with a constant formula drip. He thought it was fun at first, but the feeling of adventure wore off quickly.

Dr. Vockley wanted to admit Adam to the Children's Hospital for more testing, so another road trip was planned. Before they left, Katie updated her readers:

> Adam's belly has been distended for about six weeks and we're not sure what is going on with his liver. We are very nervous about this, and we could use all the prayers people out there can give us. We will be so far from home, and hate having Adam in the hospital anyway. It's hard to leave home on Monday and tell the five children left behind we don't know when we will be back.

Shortly after Katie and Joe were married, Joe had a chance to learn the roofing business and after much thought and prayer decided to start his own small company. Most of his work was in new construction but the housing market was slowing down and work was scarce. Joe could now leave as needed, but it also meant pay checks were not coming in as needed.

Adam was admitted to the hospital in Pittsburgh, and plans were made for an overnight fasting challenge. He would be taken off all feedings, and his blood sugar monitored closely to see how long it took for his body to go into crisis, and hopefully why that happened. The doctors would also like to do a muscle biopsy and an open liver biopsy of their own. That meant a hospital stay of at least five days, and that time estimate was only if everything went well.

The first night was very rough. Repeated attempts to insert an IV failed. Eventually, an ICU doctor came down about 2:00 a.m. and put the IV in Adam's neck. The fasting challenge had lasted only five hours when his blood sugar dropped to twenty nine, he was then in enough of a crisis state that the necessary tests could be obtained. The tube feedings were started again, and his sugar level rose quickly.

Surgery for both biopsies was scheduled for the next day with general anesthesia. Hopefully, it would not cause vomiting, which interfered with blood sugar levels, his mother whispered, words taking the shape of a tearful prayer. She added that his little toes were like pin cushions with all the pokes that were given to test his sugar.

Well, sometime during the night, Adam's IV came out and attempts to put it back in were unsuccessful. The surgeon wanted him to fast before surgery, and of course he couldn't; so they needed to get glucose in him with an IV. It appeared the doctors were unable to agree amongst themselves as to what to do, and Katie and Joe voiced their desire that Adam be sedated before anymore IV attempts. It was explained that would interfere with the anesthesia for surgery. Eventually, an IV was put in using an ultrasound and that one lasted a few hours. When Katie had the chance, she wrote on CarePages:

Now Adam's arm is full of the fluid that drained into his tissues instead of the vein. He is in quite a bit of pain from so many pokes and IV attempts. Surgery for today is cancelled, because without an IV, he can't tolerate any kind of fast. The staff tossed around the idea of putting in a more permanent line, but can't, and won't, do it on a child that is not sedated, and he can't be sedated without fasting. So here we go with our ongoing circle of problems and complications. Everyone seems to understand now that he can't fast, has no vein access, and needs surgery, but no one knows what to do about it. They are going to attempt an IV one more time in the morning, and we hope surgery will be able to get him in as an addition to the schedule.

With all the disasters of today, we are fighting hard to resist the impulse to pack up and leave. The geneticist seemed to be reading our thoughts and reminded us that the biopsy needs to be done within forty eight hours of the fasting challenge, in order to get the best information about his disorder.

As Katie and Joe prepared to spend a very long, sleepless night next to Adam's bed, they were emotionally drained and physically exhausted. They watched him as he finally was able to sleep; tearful prayers were sent to Heaven in one loud cry asking, "Please let things come together tomorrow."

The new day did bring new solutions. Adam went to radiology and a central line was put in his groin area, allowing fluids to be administered without an IV. He was also given medication to help him relax a little bit, and there were some lighter moments, when the medication caused him to giggle off and on. Taking time for a morning message, Katie wrote:

Everyone with whom we have come in contact this morning, was full of apologies for the way things were handled yesterday. It seems that all the right people are now on top of things, and we feel more confident. So the prayers of tired, scared parents were heard, and quickly acted upon. We also know the prayers were multiplied many times over by those praying for us at home.

During the surgery a mediport was installed under Adam's skin. A catheter connected the port to a vein, and the port has a septum, through which drugs could be injected and blood samples could be drawn as needed. The port was inserted in the upper chest, just below the collar bone. The doctors felt he was too unstable to send home without some vein access. It could become a life threatening situation if he was to become ill and there was any delay starting an IV. Using their long hours of waiting over the weekend, Katie updated family and friends:

> The doctors have managed to scare us, as far as how serious they think Adam's disorder is. We just wish they could learn more, and learn it quickly. We have learned that as frustrating as it is, we can't control the events around us, or make them happen on our timetable. So we ask the Lord to take care of Adam, help the doctors make the best decisions, and leave all things for Him to decide on what timetable they be done.

Surgery was completed that Monday morning, going a bit longer than planned. Due to the appearance of Adam's liver, the surgeon asked a specialist to come in and consult. Later the specialist was able to confirm Adam's belly was full of fluid due to the poorly functioning liver.

The first night after the surgery was difficult. The nurse wanted to put an oxygen mask on Adam for the night because his level with just room air had dropped, but he was not cooperating. Joe took the mask and held it about an inch from his son's face all night long and in the morning remarked to Katie, "There is no way in this world I would have been able to do that without prayers, and the hand of the Lord holding my hand in place." As he was weaned from the morphine, Adam's breathing improved. He was in an incredible amount of pain, but his parents labeled him a real trooper. The next day, after a much better night, they were on their way home, and Adam bounced back quickly once his tube feedings were restarted.

Just as Katie and Joe were thinking how good it was to be home, hugging all the kids, and settling into a routine, they were back in the hospital and Katie wrote:

I should know by now, that routine and normal, are no longer words that apply to our lives. After one night at home, Adam's incision site was having some problems. At least we are in Grand Rapids and can run home if needed. Adam is doing pretty well considering he is back in the hospital. However, he is not so polite and charming to the staff anymore. He has gotten pretty grouchy lately, and we don't blame him. We're a little grouchy too. After one day in the hospital, with no signs of fever or infection, we were sent home. We also learned some very early liver biopsy results are back and show definite cirrhosis, indicating the function of Adam's liver is declining quickly. He needs a transplant soon. Joe and I will be tested, to see if one of us might be a match for a live liver transplant, thus eliminating the wait for a donor.

Chapter 5

So the long process of preparing for surgery began. The insurance company considered Children's Hospital of Pittsburgh to be a center of excellence and, therefore, would provide more coverage than if the transplant were done elsewhere.

The next step was to schedule a transplant evaluation. During a five day period, Adam would be tested from head to toe, which fortunately could be done on an outpatient basis. As plans were being made for the trip, one conversation with the transplant team surprised Katie and she remarked excitedly to Joe, "I can barely keep up with how quickly things can change for us as we learn more. It seems the only requirement for a donor, in terms of blood, is that the blood types match. That means since mine is the same as Adam's I could be the donor." So Katie would also be tested from head to toe during the visit to Pittsburgh. If she were to fail even one of the tests, all further testing would be stopped.

Labs were first, and Katie passed them and the heart evaluation easily. Imaging of the liver showed a good shape and size for donating, but a biopsy would be required. Katie was told her liver would regenerate and return to normal size two weeks after surgery. Since none of Adam's testing was invasive, nothing upset him too much on this trip.

Enjoying a little time to relax and play with Adam, Katie and Joe caught a glimpse of Dr. Vockley just as he turned the corner and started down the hall towards them. The so familiar knots in the pit of their stomachs began to grow again. There must be a special reason for this visit, and sure enough Dr. Vockley was there to confirm a diagnosis made through the results of the muscle and liver biopsies. The official diagnosis is mitochondrial electron chain transport complex I, II, and III deficiency. It basically was a defect in the way Adam's body metabolized and converted energy. It explained his fatigue and rapid liver deterioration; in fact, the doctor confirmed he was in liver failure. Adam's kidneys were affected a little and a deficiency showed up in his muscles too. A liver transplant would fix his liver, but not the problem; the disease would not damage a new liver because the liver has its own mitochondria. There were other malfunctioning mitochondria in the rest of his cells, especially the muscle related ones and some in the brain cells. Because Adam had shown few symptoms in the muscle area, Dr. Vockley believed the liver transplant would buy him at least three years before any other symptoms presented. There was little time to absorb this new information, as the transplant team wanted a CT scan. One of Adam's labs indicated high levels of an enzyme which when elevated usually represented there was a tumor or an organ that was regenerating itself. The liver specialist thought a tumor was unlikely, but they needed to be sure. Since sedation was required and he cannot fast, a glucose IV would be started.

Adam and Katie's tests were scheduled at just about the same time. As Joe kissed them both, he was praying for strength and wisdom to make the right decisions as they moved forward. The imminent questions facing them were when should the transplant be done, and should Katie be the donor. The doctors admitted they didn't know how long Adam could wait for the transplant. He may be able to go six months, or he could start having serious trouble next week. After being told that the transplant surgery and recovery would require a stay in Pittsburgh of two to three months, and while thinking about that overwhelming prospect, Katie faced her last test, which ironically was the psychological evaluation. But the psychologist said Katie passed, and that she considered was a miracle in itself.

While reading a *Blue's Clues* book to Adam on their last night in Pittsburgh and hoping the story about bedtime would put Adam in the mood, Katie was startled when the phone rang. The transplant coordinator reported the team had met about Adam. There were no signs of improvement in the liver, so they wanted a repeat CT scan in three weeks and another lab test on the elevated enzymes. If the blood levels went up, they'd assume there was liver cancer and then would do a biopsy to confirm. If the enzyme levels were lower, they would put Adam on the transplant list. The other option was to schedule the surgery with Katie as the donor, if her biopsy results come back okay. If liver cancer was found they would not do the transplant because these tumors tend to reoccur quickly, and with the immunosuppressant drugs Adam would be on, tumors would thrive.

Katie wrote an emotional message on CarePages:

We are asking our prayer warriors to storm Heaven, as we are facing a long, stressful three weeks. It seems like an impossible situation. One outcome has us putting Adam and the whole family through a difficult major surgery, and the other outcome is worse. By the time they have these test results, we hope to have the genetic tests back on Adam and me. It may help with some decisions. One thing that does not fit with the doctor's expectations is Adam's mental state. He is very bright, observant, and talkative.

Adam's repeat CT scan was scheduled for mid June in Grand Rapids. During the week prior to the scan the labs were checked for alpha-fetoprotein (AFP), the elevated enzyme. He would be hospitalized since he needs an IV to get him through the six-hour fasting period. The doctors had also put him on several more vitamins, which hopefully would slow the progression of the disease in his muscles.

The repeated blood tests showed the enzyme levels were way over what is considered high, but even so there was a slight decline.

Two days prior to the scan, family and friends planned a mass for Adam, with a prayer service following. He remained still and peaceful in Joe's arms, as so many people reached out to touch him. It was obvious he could feel the Holy Spirit.

When writing about the evening, Katie said:

> I have to admit I was praying for a healing of his body that night. We were asking everyone we could reach to please nag God about our little boy. It works on us as parents, and we've heard it can also have the same effect on God. But as always we add to that; thy will be done, Father.

Adam handled his overnight stay in the hospital beautifully. The doctors could not give a definitive answer on any tumors, because they did not have the last scan for comparison. It depended on whether there were any changes in the nodules seen in Pittsburgh. So the disc of the scan was sent to Pittsburgh for evaluation.

Ten days later the transplant surgeon called with the news that, "Not much has changed between Adam's two scans." However, there are dark spots on the liver, so they still could not rule out cancer. They wanted to do a laparoscopy, to look for any sign of tumors outside the liver.

Adam's laparoscopy was scheduled for Friday, July 13. With a smile Katie told family, "We were able to get in fairly quickly only because three other families turned the date down due to superstition.

See how the Lord works. Now we pray for good results and a smooth procedure for Adam."

Shortly before the laparoscopy, news came from Pittsburgh regarding Adam's genetic tests. They found the defect was in his nuclear DNA, which meant he received a bad copy of the gene from both of his parents. They were carriers, but Katie should have enough healthy enzyme activity in her liver and would be a good donor.

The laparoscopy results were good, and no cancer was detected. The surgeon did biopsy in a few areas, but the transplant coordinator called a week later to say everything overall looked good for Adam. They were putting him on the transplant list, but he did not rank very high yet, because the formula used to score patients was based on things that were not that bad on Adam. The surgeon requested extra points for him, due to the value lab usually indicative of tumors being so high and his metabolic disorder. They seemed to think he would be approved for the extra points and would then move much higher up the list, but this all takes time.

Katie confided on CarePages:

We are still struggling with whether I should be the donor. There is so much to consider, and we hardly know where to start praying for some guidance. The wait for a donor could be very long. We thought the transplant would originally take place this summer, but now it will be at least fall. I will not be able to start school for some time, and if I am the donor I won't be with my baby after his surgery. But if this is the option to save his life, everything else is reduced to trivial.

So, the commitment to do the transplant with Katie as the donor was made. The surgery date, given by the transplant team, was

September 12. Katie, Joe, and Adam were to leave for Pittsburgh on September 10, and Adam would be admitted to Children's Hospital on the 11th. Their thoughts now centered on how a family of eight prepared to embark on such a monumental undertaking.

Chapter 6

One Friday night in August, while watching Andy test the balancing power of Legos and half heartedly reading the news of the day, Joe heard the phone ring. Katie will get it he thought. Soon he heard her say yes a couple of times and maybe an okay during a pretty short conversation. Returning to the living room and shaking with excitement mixed with disbelief, Katie looked at Joe and said, "How fast could you be packed and ready to go to Pittsburgh? There is a deceased donor they think would be a good match for Adam, but we have to leave within the hour." With virtually no time to think, or make plans, they decided to go for it. With a quick call to Katie's mother telling her the news and asking her to please take care of the kids, they began getting ready to leave.

After pulling random clothes from the drawer and calling it packing, making sure they had Adam's essentials, including a pillow and blanket for the car, and spreading lots of kisses all around, they were out the door. Joe's head was suddenly filled with many concerns that were probably too late to do anything about. What are we thinking? Did we pack anything we might actually need? There are bills to pay, the lawn needed cutting, and I hope I have enough money for gas. But here we are heading for Pittsburgh, driving through the night, to what we hope is the answer for Adam. Looking at Katie, Joe could see she was ecstatic thinking she would be with her baby after surgery, and all the days to follow instead of recuperating in a separate hospital. Joe decided to start the car. They made the trip in a record seven hours.

As the nurse settled Adam into the hospital bed and started an IV, they waited for the results of some pre-surgery blood tests. Suddenly, an imposing presence, in the form of a doctor Katie and Joe had never seen before, appeared in the doorway. Speaking abruptly he said, "The liver went to someone else; there will be no transplant tonight, and you should go home." Later reliving the night for family and friends, Joe said, "I sat there trying to take it all in, and I'm pretty sure I didn't say anything. It could have been that I was afraid of what might come out, or maybe I was just numb at what we had been through; I don't know."

Eventually they found out that Adam had been the back-up plan in case the scheduled recipient was not a good match. So once again their thoughts swirled as their conversation centered around what to do. "Do we stay in the Pittsburgh area? Adam is obviously high on the transplant list. Is that the no sleep talking? After all, how can we just leave our kids at home and live in Pittsburgh for who knows how long?" Emotionally they were drained, but to see how physically hard it was for Adam clarified everything. So they gathered up what little they had brought and started for home. It was in their first clear thinking moments that they decided this test run would be just that; a lesson sent from God to cement their belief that the scheduled surgery was the way to go. On the way home, Katie and Joe prayed for the little one year old, who had been the donor that night, and his family.

Chapter 7

The next three weeks were a series of planning and more planning for the time to be spent in Pittsburgh for the transplant surgery. Joe was filled with worry as he contemplated all the known facts. He thought about being a self-employed roofer and not having to ask for time off. Of course without him working, the much needed checks were not coming in to pay the bills. He knew the children would be well cared for by their grandmother, and many people had offered to bring groceries and meals to the house. A couple of neighbors had offered to take care of the lawn and do any repairs that became necessary. "As long as I am worrying," Joe continued, "I should think about the basket in the kitchen." He had set it up for mail and bills to be sorted by Grandma into folders of what would be paid now and what could wait until next month. But with no money coming in, he knew some bills would never see the inside of a folder.

Once Katie recovered, the mail and bills would be sent to them to take care of. With their laptop computer they would be able to communicate via CarePages and e-mail. One more thought went through Joe's head. He had followed The University of Michigan Wolverines for many years and now he would be spending football season in a hospital. So he had to wonder is there football in there?

Katie was also busy with her own preparations. She began getting medical records together, for Adam and herself, and organized the school work for the kids, so they would not fall too far behind during this time. Katie has home-schooled the children since Joey was in the first grade. Katie's mother could follow the lesson plans and get them started each morning doing their work. The rest would have to wait. A note was written allowing Grandma to authorize medical treatment for the children in her care, if necessary, and on top of this, Katie was trying to pack everything they could possibly need for a three month stay.

All right, is that it? Joe wondered, but before an answer took shape, his cousin called and wanted to discuss a plan. Later, Joe revealed the plan on CarePages:

> It turns out my aunt, three cousins, my sister, and one of Katie's sisters have been working out details of a care and travel plan. They have formed rotating teams traveling to Pittsburgh to care for Katie beginning the day of surgery. After a few days, another team will arrive and the previous one departs for home.

> The first group will check into the hotel where we are staying, will rotate duty times, and sleep there when not at the hospital. Whichever team is on duty when Katie is discharged from the hospital, will take her back to the hotel and care for her there. Where do people like this come from? That's right, another blessing from God.

The period of time, from early September through the second of October, is known as the birthday season for this family. Jacob would turn seven, Adam would celebrate his third birthday shortly after surgery, and Andy would turn nine while they were in Pittsburgh. Joe's two sisters each have a child with a birthday during this time as well. The family celebrated with one large party a week before surgery. Adam had a chocolate cake and, with a proud smile, blew out his three candles. That was the end of his interest in the cake, as he quickly moved on to the pile of presents.

Another part of the great master plan had Grandma driving the remaining five children to Pittsburgh after the surgery. They would stay with their parents in the hotel, when Katie was well enough to have a seven year old climb onto her lap. It did not take long to realize being away from them, for possibly three months, was out of the question. That meant leaving their eleven passenger van for Grandma and driving her minivan to Pittsburgh.

As Joe once again tried to determine if they were now prepared, he allowed himself the brief worry of how they would have worked it out if the kids had been in a traditional school.

Monday morning, September 10, with the van parked in front of the house, Joe stood in the driveway watching his family. It was an unseasonably warm end-of-summer day with a cloudless blue sky featuring nothing but sun. Nobody here was noticing the weather. Katie was fighting back tears and swallowing continuously as if pushing down all the emotions she couldn't give in to. Five darling faces waited expectantly for kisses and hugs as they clustered in the grass near the van. Joey, age fourteen, and Aaron, age twelve, may have been the only children to really understand their mother was having major surgery too. Jackie, now ten, was speaking animatedly to Adam. She told him, "What a fun trip," he was going to take in Grandma's car. Adam thought this was a lark and didn't really care where they went, as long as it was in Grandma's car. Andy and Jacob just wanted lots of kisses, as their four little arms encircled their mother's waist, seemingly unable to let go. Somehow they got through the emotionally charged goodbye session. Amid constant chants of, "I will miss you," and after promising to call them while on the road, Katie and Joe hurried into the car, because the time had come that it was no longer possible to fight back the tears.

As Adam slept, Katie watched the long stretch of endless highway and turned her thoughts to what lay ahead. What will this be like for Joe? She wondered. He's so strong, but his job as caregiver and protector of the family in these unfamiliar surroundings will test that strength. I've always loved his sense of humor and ability to see fun everywhere, but I'm having a little difficulty seeing how even Joe can keep his sense of humor behind the hospital walls.

They emerged from the Fort Pitt Tunnel just as the sun slipped behind the cityscape, offering a sky of blue nestled below wide swaths of pink; a truly gorgeous welcome. Shortly after, they got their first look at what was to be their home, or at least home base, for quite a while, Forbes Avenue Suites, located at the corner of Forbes Avenue and Halket Street, and six blocks from the Children's Hospital. The three story building was filled with small apartments and was often used by families involved in some way with the hospital. Also, the hotel usually provided a discount to those families who had loved ones staying at the hospital.

In addition to the three stories, the lower level was furnished with washers and dryers where occupants had the chance to do their own laundry on site. The main floor lobby provided service for incoming and outgoing mail, and coffee and tea were available all day. A short flight of stairs lead to the second floor where Katie and Joe's suite was located. They had three bedrooms, a full bathroom, a living room, and a kitchen, which included a small eating area. The kitchen would be put to good use as they could eliminate the cost of eating out. This should be a great location to accommodate all the families' coming and going, Joe thought. He noticed there were several suites facing the inside hall of the building and a row of apartments with doors leading to an outside walkway. This walkway, which was enclosed by a low wall topped with a railing, resembled a large balcony. Another flight of stairs lead to the third floor and additional apartments.

Preparing to spend the night, Joe knew it might be his last for a long time to sleep in a real bed. As Adam played hide and seek in the drapes, Katie called the kids at home to say good night. Finally, they unpacked and tried to tell themselves they were organized and ready for the upcoming weeks.

The next morning, as Joe entered the long driveway leading from Fifth Avenue to the door of the hospital, he began thinking about the complex world he was about to enter. Children's Hospital was part of a large medical community, known as University of Pittsburgh Medical Center (UPMC). Children's Hospital was founded in the late 1800s, when an eight story structure called the DeSoto Building was built in the Oakland area of Pittsburgh. It included a cafe, gift shop, and chapel. The north and south wings, referred to as the Silver Building, were added in the 1950s and a ten story main tower, known as the Purple Building, was added in 1986. The main tower had a rooftop heliport and was home to the emergency medicine department. Also included in this building, was a two-story subterranean parking garage. Children's Hospital began merging with UPMC in 2001 and became a specialty hospital treating infants and children. About 500,000 children a year come through the doors of Children's Hospital, Joe thought, as he wondered how he would find his way around. UPMC is one hospital with two buildings, and it was in the second building, Montefiore Hospital, that Katie was to have her surgery. This is where transplantation pioneer, Thomas Starzl, perfected transplant surgery. The hospitals were all connected by a series of pedestrian bridges and Children's Hospital could be accessed through the second and fourth floors.

Joe's thoughts returned to more immediate worries as they were led to Adam's room. No way around it, he thought, it would be a long hike from Adam to where Katie would be. Will I ever be able to leave Adam's side to be with her? I know she will have loving family surrounding her, but she is my wife. He put his mind to rest by remembering Adam must be his first consideration, and that they each had a job here. Katie was to have the surgery, and he was the caregiver.

As last minute pre-surgery testing was done, Adam discovered the buttons on his bed. He didn't seem to have a care in the world as he raised and lowered the head and played with the side rails. Just before midnight, Katie held Adam and pretty much smothered him with kisses, then left to be admitted to Montefiore Hosptial. On her way, she made one quick stop to update CarePages. She let everyone know there were four churches at home, where masses had been scheduled for Adam and her the following morning-one before and three during the surgeries. She asked those who could not attend to "Please say a prayer."

Chapter 8

The first team of caregivers was in place as dawn broke, and Katie was taken to surgery. Start time was 6:30 a.m. Her liver must be visually checked and certified acceptable before the doctors would begin on Adam. During the surgery, a piece of Katie's liver was to be placed in a cooler and walked from Montefiore Hospital to the waiting surgeons at Children's Hospital. As the day went on, things proceeded well and Adam's eight-hour surgery began at 7:50 a.m., with Dr. George Mazariegos as lead surgeon. And so it happened, on September 12, two days before his third birthday, Adam's mother gave him life again when one-third of her liver was transplanted into his small body.

So here I am, Joe thought, as he alternately paced and tried to rest, praying for my family and waiting for results of both surgeries. It was almost 9:00 p.m. before he could take out the laptop and begin an update for family and friends:

> Both Katie and Adam are in ICU beds, and doing okay. I was able to see Katie twice today; she is in a lot of pain, but I could tell her Adam is doing well. The doctors say his liver has already started to function and the next 48 hours are big. I left her in the care of not only the staff, but what I am calling my hospital angels; the small group of family, from home, determined to make this ordeal less of an ordeal.

Joe spent his first night pacing around the ICU absolutely sure he was needed to do something, anything. No, it looked like the doctors and nurses knew what they were doing without me, he concluded, as he found a quiet chair and spent the rest of the night in prayer.

Morning came, and day one of recovery began. Joe was on the laptop with an update by early afternoon:

I saw Katie this morning and she is pushing her little button for pain meds often. Seems the epidural did not function after surgery, and now she is a little nauseated from the medication. Her spirits are up though, and she is being closely monitored. Our little buddy, Adam, had some trouble during the night with his sugar levels, but that is now under control. Just before noon his breathing tube was removed, and he is doing a little talking, such as demanding the light on. He wants water, and is given a little sponge on a stick to suck on. The morphine lets him get a little rest, as he is in a lot of pain, but so far his liver numbers are great, and recovery is proceeding well.

Later in the evening, Joe posted another update telling readers:

Katie's NG tube was removed, and her pain medication was changed enabling her to sip some ginger ale. This news is transmitted to me through my hospital angels, as I have not been able to get back to see her today. The reason for that is Adam will not rest for more than 10 to 20 minutes at a time. He has managed to dislodge one drain tube, (that's why the doctors say they put in two) and has rolled over in spite of my firm restraint. He is sucking on every sponge offered to him, and seems to have a determination that I can only believe will get us out of here soon. With all that is going on, this update took an hour to write. I will talk to you all tomorrow, on Adam's third birthday. We should have some party.

As Joe closed the laptop for the day and pushed back the recliner, he thought to himself, because we are here, he will have many more birthdays.

Day two of recovery brought a birthday that was anything but fun. Joe opened the laptop in the middle of the afternoon and began:

Both Katie and Adam are in a great deal of pain. I have not been able to see Katie since yesterday morning, but, as always, my hospital angels keep me informed. I wish I could be with her and hold her hand, but Adam is not sleeping well and was finally given a sedative at 2:00 a.m. The morphine was not keeping him settled, and I could not get them to up his dose, and let me tell you I did try! Anyway the chloral hydrate worked, and we both finally got some sleep. He has been asking for me to hold him, but I cannot do that yet. However, since he has been big enough to reach up and touch the ear of the person holding him; he found comfort in holding and rubbing the earlobe. So, I lean over the bed, offer the ear, and he goes back to sleep.

Day three of recovery brought an upgrade for Adam to the open intermediate ICU ward. The blood work numbers, as well as today's ultrasound, all looked good. Joe's daily update began:

Adam is resting a lot more, and when he is awake it is for longer periods of time; a good 3 to 5 seconds. He is in a lot of pain, cannot stand the NG tube, and they had to put the nasal oxygen back in. The nurse was just letting it blow by his nose, but his numbers started to drop. I did see Katie this morning, when I was kicked out for the changing of the nurses from 7:00 to 8:00. She is in a lot of pain too, having already been up in a chair today. The pain made conversation difficult. Well, Adam is starting to moan so I better go. I would love to turn on the television and watch U of M vs. ND, but I cannot handle any more stress today.

Day four of recovery started out well. Joe's update on CarePages began late in the afternoon:

Katie was moved to a private room, and her epidural was removed. She even walked to the bathroom. She is not able to travel by wheelchair to see Adam; maybe tomorrow. This is the nightmare she envisioned for herself, not being able to touch her baby. But when you deliver on a miracle as big as this one, what's one more day? Oh, my hospital angels are happy too. Until now, they had to sit and sleep in folding chairs. Not much sleeping going on there, I would say, but Katie's private room comes with a recliner. Adam's day also brought good things. His ultrasound looked good, and the liver numbers looked so good they are moving his labs to every eight hours. His NG tube was removed, as well as one of the IV lines. The foley catheter was also removed; so far the only thing I had a little trouble watching. Did you know they blow up a little balloon, on the end, to keep it in place? None of this made him very happy, but he does have fewer things protruding from his body. I have become one of the medical community now, and I have started keeping my own medical records. I record all the medications Adam gets, and when, as well as any reactions to them. I monitor the IV's, and procedures, and which doctors come by. I know when he slept, and for how long.

Adam has been watching a little television today (NASCAR, football, oh yeah some cartoons). Yesterday's football results, 38-0, have lifted my spirits. Go blue. Talk to you all tomorrow.

Day five of recovery brought Katie, in a wheelchair, to visit Adam for a short time. She was able to hold his hand and tell him how much she loved him. Joe reported on CarePages:

Adam was not awake at the time of his mother's visit, because he had been given a sedative. His anti-rejection drug levels are too high, and causing jerking movements which wake him frequently. A chest x-ray today showed some water in his right lung, which they say is normal, and he was given more Lasix to help remove the fluid. This is the point where I start asking for extra prayers that we are able to stay away from a chest tube. The word is overall he is doing well, but some of these normal things are getting a bit hard. Adam needs to go back to the operating room to reclose the muscles in his abdomen. The surgeon only closed the skin, and had to wait for the swelling to go down to finish the job. I have known this for a couple of days, but I just didn't think you could handle it yet, so I held back on this information. The surgeon says, no big deal, normal liver transplant stuff. Stay strong and remember to pray.

As Joe finished his update, he thought, I mean that as much for myself as for them.

Day six of recovery arrived and Katie was discharged. Before leaving, she used the hospital's computer to do her own update:

Adam's surgery to reclose the muscles went well. They may have to go in one more time down the road, and finish closing his muscles, but maybe not; sometimes they close on their own. I have learned tips on getting out of bed and generally getting around. It feels so good to have all the tubes and wires out.

Later in the day, Joe was able to confirm:

My hospital angels have taken Katie back to the hotel. I am so grateful to them, at least I know she is cared for. How did we think we could have done this alone? A new team of helpers arrived; the first group has gone home.

Once back at the hotel while trying to eat, and borrowing her hospital angel's laptop, Katie wrote:

I am so grateful for the wonderful messages and prayers. They carry us through those many days, when we just do not have the strength to pray. There have been some very dark nights, and I know things can and will get better. I ache to be with Adam and hold him, but Joe and I decided it will upset him too much for me to be there when he is awake. He would want me to hold him, or lean over him so he can take my ear. I can't do that yet. I was thinking how he must be wondering where I have been, and how I could have abandoned him at this time when he needs me most. And of course God hit me between the eyes with the knowledge that I have felt that way about God for the last several months, as we prayed for the miracle healing that never happened. I admit I felt God had forsaken me, and did not know why. I still do not know the why part, but I know that the best thing I could do for Adam is to stay away and heal, while he is well cared for by his daddy. I miss the other kids more than I can manage most nights and cannot wait to kiss each of them. Christ will use all of this for good, and He is always there for me. In His silence I must look harder for Him, and I will never be the same once this is done. I know calling Him silent makes no sense, because He speaks to us through all of you. He knows how weak I am, and that without your words I would not live up to His plan. I ask for your prayers for Joe that he can get some sleep. He is a rock and I am so proud of him, but even rocks rest a lot.

Day seven of recovery and Joe wrote:

The world looks pretty good to me right now, because I got some sleep last night. One of the hospital angels would not leave until I took a nice long nap. She sat at Adam's bedside and watched over him. I needed it too, because Adam was in a lot of pain after the surgery to close the muscles. He would wake up and shake violently. I asked everyone, including the cleaning people, how can we get poor Adam to sleep? Everyone said the same thing; he is in pain and needs more morphine. Research revealed morphine to have side effects such as twitches, and sweating; so he was changed to Dilaudid which has the same side effects, just not as bad. He was able to rest then, at least enough for me to find a semi quiet place to sleep. I found an empty gurney in the hallway and pulled a sheet over me. A casino has less noise than this place. I will end my evening with the promise to pray for all of you who listen to me on CarePages.

Day eight of recovery brought a quiet room and problems, as Joe talked about his day:

We were moved to a nice quiet room on the seventh floor, which is the transplant floor. It has several chairs, and not one but two, that fold down into beds. I moved mine as close as I could to Adam's bed, and even got a pillow, sheets, and a blanket. That is when things started to go wrong. The nurse tried to start his feedings using a slow drip, and the vomiting began. It was pretty consistent, and after several hours, the doctors concluded he has pancreatitis. The amylase and lipase enzymes are a little high. Because the pancreas goes into action when a person eats, he should get better with no tube feeding for a few days. The pancreas needs to rest. This happens sometimes because of manipulation during surgery. In addition, they believe he has a condition which is a temporary arrest of the intestinal peristalsis. It occurs most commonly after abdominal surgery. The symptoms include nausea, vomiting, and vague abdominal discomfort. They all say a few days of not eating or drinking should do the trick. I need to read the prayers and wishes sent in on CarePages often on a day like this.

Chapter 9

Day nine of recovery brought the family together and Joe wrote:

> After a doctor's appointment at the hospital, Katie was able to spend all afternoon with Adam and me. It was so good for her to touch Adam, and he even laughed a little. He is still battling pancreatitis, so no water, and it is heart wrenching when he asks for it. We need to get him moving a little, to give the muscles a work out and ease some of the pain. Katie has one more doctor's appointment left next week, and then her part will be completed.

Day ten of recovery started with Adam needing blood to treat anemia. Joe was also able to give some good news:

> The doctor took the central line out of Adam's neck. I know that has been bothering him, and should make him more comfortable. His pancreas numbers are down nicely, and if they continue to go down, feedings will be given through his tube tomorrow. I took a little time to indulge in my favorite pastime today, but I have to say this quietly, as we are in Pennsylvania, U of M over Penn State, 14-9. Go blue.

Day eleven of recovery brought in blood cultures to check for infection as Adam began running a slight fever. Joe explained on CarePages:

> The fever began last night, so they even cut off the tip of the central line, removed yesterday, to be tested. His blood cultures have been negative so far, but they will grow for five days. Today is Sunday, and according to my records, it is time to change the IV and dressing day. Oh, Adam is going to love that! He has just recovered from removal of the central line.

The last team of hospital angels left for home, as Katie's sister arrived from Chicago. Reading to Adam, from his recliner turned bed, Joe stood when he heard Katie and Kelly enter the room. He kissed them both, told them to have a wonderful visit with Adam, and left for mass in the hospital chapel. A chance to leave the room for any reason was rare, and he was looking forward to going to mass.

Day twelve of recovery and it is a Monday. Joe did not get a chance to update CarePages until evening:

> Monday, Monday, I am not sure how to start this one. One of Adam's cultures came back positive for a yeast infection from the Mediport line. What that means, I really don't know. They took more blood from the line to run a new culture, and gave him an anti-fungal treatment through his IV line that took four hours. There will be a second treatment tomorrow. They will keep running cultures, to see if the treatments are working. His monitor was removed; probably got sick of it going off all the time. On a positive note, Adam's pancreas numbers are down and

a slow drip was started. Adam did have some fun today after his mother sent me to the cafe to eat. She said some lady with a guitar stopped by, and Adam smiled, sat up for awhile, played with some toys, and is now babysitting some frog for the lady. I'm going to have to take her word for it, but he just asked me for his medicine so who knows what happened here. Adam's hair was washed today, and he looks a lot better. Thanks to all of you for listening to my world.

Day thirteen of recovery and Katie was at the hotel enjoying a rare chance to laugh. She used her sister's laptop to clarify the events of yesterday:

I just read Joe's update from last night, and thought I could interpret a little. A woman from music therapy paid a visit to Adam, and he responded very well to it. She showed him several instruments, and his favorite was one shaped like a frog. She told him he could take care of it for her until next time. After that, he seemed to remember there are still good things in life, started asking for toys and actually enjoyed playing for quite a long time. It was so good to see him smile and have fun. He still gets irritable often, but we will take all the good times we can get.

At the hospital, Joe's update began early in the evening:

Good evening. Katie let me out for food again today, while she took Adam to the play center. It is almost across the hall, and he seemed to enjoy the variety of toys. When the center closed, I walked Adam in the halls for several hours, while Katie attended a meeting about what to do after Adam is discharged. She is now concerned about what we will do if we have to come back here as often as the speaker said situations would force us to. Adam is still cranky and irritable, and the doctors say it is caused by the anti-rejection meds, and/or anti-fungal meds. It could just be post surgery, or just being three. Bedtime has been later and later, and I hope as we walk the halls that tonight it can be before 1 a.m. His feedings have been bumped up slightly, to a whopping two teaspoons per hour. So far he is tolerating it. As I head back to his room, I pray for a peaceful evening, where Adam is not worried or scared, or making me read the same book 6,000 times.

Day fourteen of recovery was not such a good day:

Adam was so irritable I walked him in the stroller, and even took a trip to the outside courtyard in back of the hospital. He was not impressed, but I was. The sky was the bluest I have ever seen, although I was squinting, having been inside so long.

I lingered as long as possible, planning a fantasy escape route, but I did not want him to fall asleep in the stroller; so we went back inside. Most nights are spent with me trying to entertain him when he cannot sleep. The doctors say if they can fine-tune his meds, they believe he will not be so crabby. I say this is something to shoot for. Katie was not able to see Adam today, because she was sick all night, and we are not sure what is going on. In addition, she is having severe shoulder pain, and during a phone call to the transplant clinic was told it may be pancreatitis. She is worried as the only way to treat that, is by eliminating anything by mouth for about three days, as they did with Adam. To avoid dehydration, she may have to be admitted to the hospital for IV fluids. Of course Katie does not want to do that, because not seeing Adam today was incredibly hard. She tearfully said she wants to rock him and snuggle him while he is having such a bad time, but now when will that be? Our other five kids are supposed to arrive this Friday, and this all really needs to be resolved by then.

Day fifteen of recovery and Joe said:

It sure feels like Monday. Katie had her staples pulled today. She has not had food or liquids since yesterday, but an ultrasound today looked good. They could not find her pancreas and do not seem worried, which all seems odd to me. She can eat now and needs her vanilla coffee. So here we go with Adam news. He was crabby last night, fell asleep about 1 a.m., and slept until the nurse woke him for his meds at 8 a.m. That is a tough time because he gets the anti-rejection med sprinkled on his tongue, and after that can put nothing in his mouth for thirty minutes. That is the time he needs his binky for comfort, and I always have to tell him I am looking for it. I did take him for a stroller ride, which he seemed to enjoy.

That is about it for the good news today. Adam's chest x-ray showed some fluid. They call it pleural effusion. The doctors are also concerned with some liver numbers that are a little out of line. They say it could be a sign of rejection. He was given some medication to help drain the fluid and tomorrow will be going back to the table to have a small catheter, slightly smaller than a chest tube, inserted to drain the fluid. Next they will do a needle liver biopsy to see what is going on and several other x-rays. He is still getting his anti-fungal treatment, with 10 days to go; even though all his cultures have been negative except for that first one. It looks like we are not getting out of here any time soon. So, I am not sure if all these pleadings are starting to bug God; so maybe you could tone it down a bit and whisper.

Day sixteen of recovery began at 3:00 a.m.:

I should have seen it coming when Adam fell asleep early in the evening. All he wanted was water today, and it broke my heart trying to distract him. The kid is so smart; he found every drinking fountain on our morning stroller ride and even started asking for coffee. This was a tough day because I thought his procedure would be done early, but the day dragged on until they took him in at 2:30 p.m. I got to carry him down to radiology, and made them suit me up so I could bring him in and try to comfort him, until he was given some medication, and then given more medication. As we learned back in our ICU days, it takes a lot to put Adam under. The procedure took about an hour and the tube seems to be working. Hopefully it will make him feel better. He is resting now but wakes often and moans, so I am not sure what kind of night it will be. We hope to have the liver biopsy results tomorrow and know if there is any rejection. I do not think there is; my records show his liver numbers have come down. We are still trying to figure out when to start his feedings, and he still needs his fungal treatment, and an x-ray at 9:00 p.m. So there is a lot of catch up to do tonight, to get him back to where he was at midnight last night.

I sense it will be a short night for me; so just a quick family update. You all remember this is the day my children were due to arrive? Well, I hear Grandma started out early this morning accompanied by her mother, who could not be left back in Michigan alone, and a close family friend to share the driving and be all around help as needed. Grandma gave each child a list of fifty things to find on the trip, and the winner picked the spot where they would all have ice cream. I have heard they had to take another apartment down the hall, as one will no longer be large enough. That must have been fun for the last angel left here. Kelly will fly out tomorrow, after getting everyone settled in their rooms.

Chapter 10

Day seventeen of recovery was a nice distraction for Adam. His four brothers, sister, and grandmother came for a visit. Between Adam's room and the hallway is a small room complete with sink, several kinds of antibacterial soap, paper towels, and a bin with disposable gloves. A window, with blinds, separates this room from the patient's room. On arrival the group was instructed to wash their hands well, which is a requirement for anyone entering the room staff and visitors. This took some time for the younger boys to grasp. "You mean even if we go out in the hall for a minute, we have to wash our hands to come back in?" Jacob was certain he must have misunderstood. The kids were able to get lots of smiles out of Adam, as Joe looked over and saw bubbles floating above his bed. Andy had snuggled up close to him, and as Joe watched with disbelieving eyes, he counted four siblings on Adam's bed. Jacob was preoccupied, for the moment, with questions about the room. Referring to extra IV tubing, assorted catheters, and syringes, he asked, "Mommy, does Adam get to play with all this stuff?" Jacob was also fascinated with Joe's self-described survival basket, which was filled with crackers, creamer, packets of sugar, salt, pepper, mayonnaise, and ketchup.

That evening during the report on his day, Joe wrote:

The doctor came in this afternoon and said yesterday's biopsy showed the beginning of a mild rejection, and so they will start him on steroids today. The transplant people do not seem very worried because they said rejections are par for the course, and this one was caught early. His mother and I hate to see him on more medications, but you do what you have to. This is wearing on my hopes, because just when things seem to improve, a new complication comes along. They may do another liver biopsy to confirm that the steroids are working, but we won't know for several days. His liver numbers are still good, but when there is even a mild sign of rejection, they do not waste time; they just treat it. Hopefully after playing with the kids today, Adam will sleep well tonight. And for all of you out there who don't know, U of M beat Northwestern, 28-16. Go blue.

Day eighteen of recovery and Adam slept until 6 a.m. Updating CarePages Joe reported:

I took Adam for a walk today, and was able to trick him into taking a few steps by putting the stroller a few feet away, and placing him on the floor carefully so he would walk to the stroller. We need to get his muscles back in shape, but Adam has no interest in that. Today was change the mediport day, which means they pull the needle and dressing, put a fresh one in, and re-tape it. Obviously he hates that and screams. His chest x-ray looked good today, so I'm hoping the chest tube will be removed soon. Katie's energy level is improving but she still cannot lift anything, and even though she wants to spend a night here with Adam; she is not ready for that. However, she is hoping to resume classes soon, as the kids brought all their books to Pittsburgh.

Day nineteen of recovery brought a conservative view on the chest tube, and it was decided that it should be left in for now. Joe let everyone know:

We tried to get Adam on a more normal eating schedule by spacing out his tube feeding, and giving more at a time, but he couldn't keep it down. They will try again tomorrow, and slow it down to a drip overnight. Is his tummy sensitive because of the surgery or from the metabolic disease? So many things will improve because of the new liver, but some of his old problems related to metabolism will remain. No one seems willing to speculate which ones.

The kids were able to come up again this afternoon, and it is amazing how they perk Adam up and get him to talk more than Katie and I ever could. I think having them here will be his best medicine. It is supposed to be in the 80s this week, and we would sure like to get him out in the fresh air.

Day twenty of recovery was Adam's best so far. Joe was able to report:

It's Andy's birthday, and since this most likely is not a perfect birthday for a nine year old, Katie brought him up for some alone time with Adam and the two of us. Adam had a total attitude change while Andy was here. Watching them play was good for us too, and Adam sat up on his own for the first time. Katie said this is a big milestone because she knows it really does hurt. Adam was able to keep all his feedings down today, and they capped off the chest catheter, but will do one more x-ray before they take it out. All of Adam's labs look good, other than the occasional vitamin/mineral deficiency, a side effect of the immunosuppressant medication. The doctors will not discuss a discharge date yet, but that's okay. I think Adam and I are going to live here and have visitors, but never be part of the outside world.

Day twenty-one of recovery found Joe struggling to remember God is in control:

It seems every time we have good news and see the light at the end of the tunnel, something goes wrong. Adam had an ultrasound this afternoon, and they found the main artery that runs to the liver has low blood flow. They need to get a better look at it, and so he will have an angiogram and another biopsy tomorrow. Jackie was not feeling well today, so Katie and I made the decision no one could visit. That was hard, but necessary. This will be our new reality; we must try to keep Adam away from illness. It is such a blessing to read our CarePages and know so many people will be praying for Adam in the morning.

Day twenty-two of recovery and Joe wrote thank you to everyone on CarePages for their continued prayers:

The angiogram went well, and it was decided a biopsy was not necessary. They needed to clear the hepatic artery with a balloon and then there was very good flow through it. The surgeons are pleased with the results, and they think the fluid he had near his lung was most likely due to the poor flow in the artery. Now that it is repaired the fluid should correct itself, and maybe that tube can come out soon. It means there may not have been any rejection going on. To keep this from happening again, Adam will need to be on a blood thinner. We will have to give him two shots a day for about six months. Late in the day, Adam started to come around and his feedings were restarted. Katie kissed us both and headed back to the hotel, as she had been away from the other kids all day.

As he started the video player, Joe thought, well, it looks like my evening is going to be a Blues Clues marathon. While Adam watched the screen intently, Joe walked to the window, looked out, and wondered just when he and Adam would breathe fresh air again.

Day twenty-three of recovery, and Adam will have another angiogram. Joe began:

This morning's ultrasound showed low blood flow again in the hepatic artery, just past where the angioplasty was yesterday. They suspect it is clotting, but will not know for sure until they get in there. If it is low flow and not a clot, then they will do the balloon procedure again. If it is clotting, they will inject a clot busting medicine, to try to break it up. Everything moved very quickly today, and we are still in shock about this turn of events. Adam has a fever, which has been steadily rising all day. The reluctance was palpable in the doctor's voice when he said, "We would normally not do an angiogram in a child with a fever, but this is an urgent procedure and the risks of not doing it are greater." It was explained to us that therapy in a highly pressurized oxygen chamber will be tried if there is no flow of blood in the artery. If this is necessary, then Adam will have a surgical procedure to place ear tubes tonight, in order for the treatments to start tomorrow.

We are not sure what to pray for specifically; we are just sure we need prayers, and are asking our prayer warriors to respond. The doctors are also checking for infection because of the fever. We are overwhelmed with worry, and feel like we are at the end of our rope. It is awful to think of Adam scared anymore, but he will come out of this procedure with another IV PICC line so they can get more labs, and give him more meds. A PICC line, is a central line placed in a peripheral vein, usually the upper arm. Pray it does not fail, like the ones have in the past.

After completion of the angiogram, Katie wrote an update on CarePages, with all the emotion she was feeling:

The angiogram showed a clot in the artery, just past the graft they used to connect my liver to him. The radiologist does not see how it can be resolved without surgery. Dr. Mazariegos wants to get an ultrasound at 7 a.m. and see how the flow responded to the clot busting meds they gave him during the procedure. If there is good flow, then all is well for now. If there is low flow, or no flow, Adam will go right to the operating room for ear tubes, and then to the hyperbaric oxygen chamber to begin two weeks of therapy. It would be twice a day, an hour each time. Joe would have to cut off one of his ears since that is Adam's comfort thing, and they do not allow parents to go into the chamber with the child. Adam is on so many drugs now; even Joe is having a hard time keeping track. He is on IV glucose, so his blood sugar is stable. No milk after midnight, in case he has to be fasting for the ear tube surgery.

We feel blind sided by all this, and Adam is simply miserable. He has several new sites that hurt, and he is so drugged up he just whimpers. He still has a fever, but they say it is from the arterial problems, and he is getting antibiotics to cover everything. It seems all we do is ask for prayers, but we just cannot utter a prayer right now without feeling a little frustrated with God's plan here. Our hearts know He is there, and taking care, but my head is screaming that Adam should not be going through any of this. This is where we depend on our prayer warriors to say the prayers we cannot and carry us through.

Finally alone with Adam, Joe sat on the edge of his bed watching over him, and touching him tenderly. Thoughts of those with whom he had entrusted his prayers ran through his mind. The last time I felt this low I called on Pope John Paul II, he recalled. After asking him again to intercede on Adam's behalf, Joe called on someone else who figured prominently in their prayers leading up to the transplant. Katie and Joe have had a strong devotion to Saint Pio, known most of his life as Padre Pio.

When Adam became ill, an aunt gave them a book detailing his amazing ability to intercede through prayer, and of the many healings, both physical and spiritual, attributed to his intercession. Katie and Joe felt his guidance as they made their way through all the tough decisions.

Francesco Forgone, named in honor of St. Francis, was born in 1887 in Pietrelcina, Italy. As a young child Francesco witnessed a healing miracle, and from then on dedicated himself to the service of the Lord, often doing harsh penance trying to become more like Jesus. He suffered poor health as a child and spent long periods in bed. Ordained a priest in 1910, Padre Pio joined the Capuchin order. In 1918, he received the visible wounds of Christ's crucifixion, becoming the first priest in the church to receive the stigmata. He bore it for 50 years until his death in 1968, sometimes enduring skeptics in his own church.

Having the gift to read what was in the heart, as well as the gift of bi-location, Padre Pio often heard confessions ten or twelve hours a day. Countless more corresponded with him to receive guidance.

In 1962, a bishop in Krakow wrote to Padre Pio asking for prayers for a young mother who was dying. Padre Pio assured him he would pray and eleven days later the woman's tumor disappeared. The young bishop, who later became Pope John Paul II, had the honor of elevating Padre Pio to sainthood in June of 2002.

Katie found a friary in Pennsylvania of the same order as Padre Pio. She wrote to the friars explaining Adam's medical condition and asked them to pray for him. She received a note back saying not only would they pray for Adam, but if it was ever possible for them to visit when in Pittsburgh, they would bless Adam and pray over him.

On one of their trips to see Dr. Vockley, Katie, Joe, and Adam did visit the friary. They were invited to dinner and afterwards taken to the chapel for a blessing, where they were given a relic of Padre Pio's, which they pinned to Adam's bed.

Since then Saint Pio has been the recipient of many requests for intercession and prayer. With his hand still on Adam, Joe finally felt enough peace to close his eyes. He knew he was not quite so alone.

Day twenty-four of recovery and the 7 a.m. ultrasound showed enough blood flow to cancel the ear tubes and oxygen chamber for now. Another ultrasound would be done in a few hours. Upon hearing the results of the second ultrasound, Joe went to the computer:

The second test showed good blood flow. The surgeon admitted he did not expect this result, and is at a loss to explain why the clot broke up so nicely. Adam will continue on blood thinners, and an ultrasound will be scheduled everyday for awhile. Due to low hemoglobin, he needed blood this afternoon and is pretty cranky, but so am I. That does not mean we have overlooked the miracle that happened here today. Feeling a little better, I allowed myself the indulgence of football while Adam slept. U of M beat Eastern Michigan, 33-32. Go blue.

Day twenty-five of recovery and Katie took my laptop:

Katie needs the laptop to help the kids with their school work. I had to hack into the nurses' computer to update my readers. I can't help it if they just leave these things lying around the room.

Getting started, we'll just call this black Sunday. Adam woke just before 7 a.m. a bit cranky and irritable, and at 8:30 threw up. I have no idea why, but the day went down from there. Katie came in after mass so I could go, but we were called down to ultrasound so that did not happen. The flow in the artery is still good, but Adam's chest tube is blocked. This means a trip to surgery tomorrow to have it replaced. His new PICC line dressing, on his arm, was changed today. Sunday is also change mediport day, which he just loves. He loved it so much he vomited half way through. Washing, and a bed change followed, after which the nurse finished her task. Adam's urine cultures came back positive for a couple of different bugs, but the two antibiotics he is on should solve that problem. I started his feedings again, along with some Zofran for the nausea, and so far so good. Tonight should be okay because he is very tired, and I do not think there is any more they can do today to cause him pain. Adam is still very cranky, and he does not want me to keep the TV on, but if I can just distract him for fifty more laps. Pray for a good Monday.

Day twenty-six of recovery and Adam was sleeping off his sedation. Joe began the daily news with an update on the morning surgery:

The chest tube was replaced, draining a liter of fluid from his chest. The surgeon said again, he can't believe how the clot dissolved so nicely, and now the chest fluid is his biggest problem. Adam is still being treated for the bugs in his urinary tract, but they should be resolved soon.

As Joe absently wandered about the room, he became acutely aware of what his life had become. As he played it over in his mind what everyone's day was like when there was no crisis, he realized somehow in a combination of accident, and organization, they had all settled into a routine.

Joe started his day looking forward to the beloved coffee cart that made its rounds about 8:00 a.m., offering parents who had not slept, a much needed refreshment. Since Katie's mother arrived, she showed up about 8:30 with breakfast. The smell of homemade English muffins, toasted, and stuffed with eggs, cheese, and bacon lingered long after breakfast was finished.

At the hotel, she prepared the food and packed it in a shoulder tote. Then she added a carton of chocolate pudding for later, or an apple and chocolate chip cookies. She walked down Forbes Avenue, stopped at the corner newspaper box and picked up a copy of USA Today to add to her tote. Turning left onto Meyran, she headed toward Fifth Avenue and crossed the street with a crowd of people headed in many directions.

Entering the hospital and signing in at the desk, she picked up her pass for the day and then headed for the first floor cafe. There she picked up a large coffee and something gooey and delicious. It was often a chocolate fudge donut with thick chocolate icing sliding down the sides, or a cherry turnover with vanilla glaze covering the still warm pastry.

After breakfast and Adam's morning medications, Joe headed to the shower next door. He could hear the water running when people showered, so he always knew when it was empty. Grandma stayed with Adam and watched Mickey Mouse Clubhouse. Sometime during the last week or so, he had discovered this show and seemed awed by the cast of characters. This was during the half hour when he could not have his binky because he just had his anti-rejection medicine; so the show had become a good distraction.

Grandma loved her visit time with Adam, and when the show was over she offered him some little surprise that they would find together in her purse. The little group often went to the playroom after this or for a walk in the hall. Every floor seemed to have countdown posters for the day when the new Children's Hospital would open. It looked like it was to happen in May of 2009. Being a stranger to Pittsburgh, Joe didn't know where Lawrenceville was, but he was pretty sure they would meet. By midmorning, after kissing Adam goodbye numerous times, Grandma took the laundry and went back to the hotel. She would stay with the kids and begin the washing, so that when Katie was ready, she could come and spend the afternoon with Adam.

During her morning, Katie had given the children their breakfast and started them on their schoolwork. She explained any new work, answered questions, and gave them various assignments to complete while she was at the hospital. On the way to the hospital, Katie passed McDonalds, and either picked up a couple of cheeseburgers for Joe's lunch, or visited the hospital cafe for ham and cheese on an onion bun and, of course, more coffee. She also brought clean clothes for the next day. Non-crisis afternoons were spent playing with Adam and trying to get him to walk.

Sometime in the early evening Joe reminisced, their good friend Pat, who traveled here with the grandmas, showed up. Katie's mom made and packed dinner, and he walked it to the hospital. "When was that?" Joe tried to remember. Yesterday or maybe the day before, the days kind of run together, but the smell of salisbury steak and mashed potatoes smothered with cracked peppercorn gravy, and green beans with caramelized onions filled the room. A banana goes into my growing survival basket. Apple pie with flaky crust and melt in your mouth cinnamon apples, was often in the dinner bag, and of course got eaten right away.

Pat waited until Katie was ready to leave for the night and walked her back to the hotel. The walking had been good for Katie, but Joe was glad she was not doing it alone at night. While here Pat taught Adam to play the card game, War, and they played it most evenings.

Great Grandma did her share of staying with the kids whenever she was called upon, and was very good at folding the laundry. Yes, they were moving along like what do they call it? Oh yes, a well-oiled machine. This seemed to be Joe's life and he did not see any changes coming anytime soon. With no exercise, except stroller walks, and the way he looked forward to meals Joe knew he would have to make up for this if he ever got out. As Joe settled against his pillows, his eyes slowly closing, he wondered both about when he and Adam would get out and whether there would be sticky cinnamon buns or chocolate donuts in the morning.

Chapter 11

Day twenty-seven of recovery and Joe began with some pessimism:

I am a little hesitant to give a good update, because they are usually followed by some problem. But we will not be pessimistic. Adam spent a lot of time today in the playroom across the hall. He even stood for several minutes. He had to hold on to me, but at least he did it. He was weighed today, and has lost three pounds since surgery; that is 10 percent of his body weight. He looks so skinny, and his little legs have hardly any muscle mass. If we can keep complications at bay, we'll focus more on getting him stronger, and bulking up his feedings so he can put on some weight. All and all a pretty quiet day, but around here that is good news. It looks like we will go home with two shots to give Adam each day. They will be switched over from IV form this week, and training for us to give the shots will begin. I am sure Adam will be just thrilled, but as long as my ear is available, he will be okay.

Day twenty-eight of recovery and Joe said:

What can I say? Adam had a so so day. The lab people woke him early to draw blood, and then I got him to sleep and x-ray came. He spent some time in the playroom this morning, but did not want to stand or walk today. The x-ray results showed a little chest fluid remains. The doctor flushed out the line, and hopefully that will help drain the fluid. I hear fall has come, and the weather has cooled. I hope we will be out of here before the snow starts. Katie was here, and she thinks it's okay for Adam to smash a Reese's peanut butter cup into his DVD player. Of course I had to be the bad guy and stop this madness. Oh, since it is a so-so day anyway, maybe we should have one of those moments when I tell you something I left out twenty-nine days ago after transplant surgery. Adam's appendix was removed during that surgery, because it was higher than normal, and the doctors were worried that sometime in the future his appendicitis might be misdiagnosed. Well, thanks for listening to this shut-in.

Day twenty-nine of recovery was a playful day, and Joe started with a happy update:

We visited the elaborate electric train several floors down. It is enclosed in glass, but low enough so a child in a stroller can see it well. Then off to the hospital library, where Adam took about twenty steps to get to the aquarium. He is shaky on his feet, but what an improvement that he even wanted to walk. His chest is still producing some fluid and the surgeon said the magic number is 100ml, or just over three ounces of output, before they can cap off the chest tube and see if it is ready to be removed. Adam's brothers and sister came to visit today, and for a while the noise and laughing felt just like home. Katie is still here, and wants to add a note.

This is just for the record. Adam was smashing a peanut butter cup into the screen of the DVD player, and it was completely washable, but dad can be so fussy. If the kid is having fun, why rock the boat? I guess it's a good thing I am not the one here twenty four hours a day.

Day thirty of recovery was education day.

Grandma brought the kids to the hospital early in the afternoon, and everyone went downstairs to pathology for a science lesson. They were shown what a healthy liver looked like first and then Adam's liver was placed next to it. His liver was full of fat and twice the size of the healthy one. Katie was heard to sigh, as she absorbed what she was seeing. "It's hard to believe that thing was in my little boy. It has such a sick appearance." This was very therapeutic, because when recovery was moving slowly and he didn't seem outwardly sick before surgery, it had been easy to doubt whether or not they had done the right thing. Now they knew for sure they did choose the right course of action. The kids did great, even put on gloves and touched the livers, except for Jacob, who was completely grossed out. Adam was not impressed either.

Getting back to medical issues, Joe did a CarePages update:

There is talk of doing another biopsy on Monday, because the chest fluid is not clearing up. But that is a problem for another day, as I'm trying to deal with those in front of me now. An attempt was made late this afternoon to take

Adam's remaining staples out. He became hysterical, so the doctor stopped, and will try again another day. I really cannot imagine Adam will be any less hysterical when they try again.

Joe also thanked everyone for his or her cards and prayers, and thought of the wonderful people who had also sent checks, knowing that during this time with no work had been difficult.
Day thirty-one of recovery and Joe wrote:

Although it is Saturday, Adam's PICC line and mediport dressings were changed, as the IV lady will not be here tomorrow. The big question today seems to be what to do with his chest tube? It is still draining and clogs often. The transplant doctor is having a hard time figuring it out, so just in case, they will check for rejection and do a biopsy on Monday. Adam's liver numbers are good, but the fluid should have stopped by now; so we will see. This will be Adam's fifth time down to the room in the corner on the fourth floor, just past Big Bird, Bert, and Ernie. He does not like the red staff elevators, because he is on to what happens when we take him there and I put on the white outfit and the blue hat. Just so you all understand I am still tuned in to the outside world,; I saw today's win over Purdue, 48-21. Go blue.

Day thirty-two of recovery is a quiet Sunday:

While Katie was here, I was able to get to mass. It made me think how much I miss our church back home, and all our friends. I prayed for all of us, and for all of you who are praying for us. Katie filled me in today on all the other families she has found through CarePages. She is especially interested in children with mitochondrial disease, and every case tugs at her heart strings. In addition to those children, she is closely following transplant patients. I wish you all a good week.

Day thirty-three of recovery and Adam seemed to be having a nice morning playing and watching videos:

He knew something was up the minute we started talking about going for a ride. He kept saying, "No pictures no pictures." He knew we were headed to radiology and some kind of test, but the biopsy went well. Even better; they were able to remove the rest of his stitches and staples, while he was sedated. Now we wait for the results. If all is okay with the liver, they will cap the chest tube and see if the fluid comes back. If it does, there will be a consultation with a specialist in this field to see what is going on. So the prayer today is the fluid goes away, and stays away. We still have six weeks of clinic visits once we are out of the hospital, and we are eager to get started so we can go home. We ask for prayers once again.

Day thirty-four of recovery and the biopsy results were back. Joe began his update with good news:

There is no sign of rejection, and the chest tube has been capped. Now we wait, and wait, and wait to see if the fluid returns. Daily x-rays will check progress. Adam's Lovenox (blood thinner) has been switched from IV form to shots. The nurse gave him his first one, and I am supposed to be watching because they actually expect me to do it soon. The needle is a lot bigger than it sounded, and it took all three of us in the room to hold him down and give the shot. I do not know how we are going to do this to him twice a day. Other than the shot, Adam had a good day doing some walking and playing.

Day thirty-five of recovery and Joe's update was delivered very late in the day:

I was going to skip this update. Even though I know everything is alright,; these Lovenox shots are not going well for Katie and me. But we will start with the good news. Today's x-ray looked good, and I think they will do one more tomorrow, and if that one is good, that stinking chest tube will be removed. Adam's x-rays are usually done in his room, but today we had to go down to fourth floor radiology. He was not happy, and I sure did a lot of comforting. He repeats often, "I do not like that room, place, elevator," or whatever the scary place of the day is. With the chest tube capped, and no cords hanging from his body, he walked to the purple elevators. He likes those, as they take us to the electric train, and from there we walked to the library. On the way back, we ventured to the main floor lobby.

Local college students are painting the windows, of the almost completely glassed in area with fun characters, to create a happy entrance to the hospital. On the other side of the glass is the driveway leading from Fifth Ave. to the main door of the hospital. It is also the driveway leading away from the main door, and I allowed myself a few minutes to daydream about that. Now about the part of the day that was not so good. Adam did not see the 6:30 a.m. Lovenox shot coming, because he was sleeping. He woke quickly and cried very hard, but I was able to get him back to sleep. His evening shot at 6:30 p.m. was not pretty at all. Both Katie and I were there for that one and it took two nurses and me, to hold him down while it was given. I have never heard him cry like he does with these shots. I will find a way to do this but it really stinks. We were given a cream to numb the skin a little, prior to the shot, but he really hates that. So in closing let me say I have spoken to one of the transplant surgeons about putting the medication in Adam's tube. He promised to research it, as older children who are on Coumadin are able to take it orally.

Day thirty-six of recovery and Joe apologized for the late update:

Giving Lovenox this morning had the same result as yesterday, then a little unexpected vomiting, and we were off to a good start. The x-ray machine came to us today and after all that, Adam was cranky and irritable. I was not doing so well either, so I put him in the stroller to do some serious traveling. Now that he has been to all the fun places in the hospital, that is all he wants to do, and boy does he tell me where we are going next. A couple of hours later, we returned to the room. We did not have to give Adam his Lovenox shot tonight. I'm sure you are asking, why Joe? Did they put him on Coumadin? No, after waiting most of the afternoon for the x-ray results, the floor doctor spoke to transplant, and we were told there is a little more fluid around the lung, and the doctors are weighing their options.

Option one is to pull the tube, and see what happens. Option two is remove the tube, and put a new one in to drain the fluid. Option three is to flush the tube, hook it back up, and try to drain the fluid. There was an option four, but by this time I was so overcome with options, I did not process that one. The winner was option three. It was flushed and nothing came out; so it is clogged. Adam will have no feedings or water after 4 a.m. tomorrow, in case the morning x-ray shows more fluid. In that case, we will go down to Adam's favorite place, fourth floor radiology, to have a new tube placed, or whatever, to get the fluid out. Oh yeah, Adam needs more blood, and will be getting that tomorrow.

Day thirty-seven of recovery and Adam's morning x-ray showed enough fluid accumulation to need his chest tube replaced, as Joe wrote in this account of the day:

There seems to be an agreement among the doctors that the current tube is not working properly. This merry-go-round we are on shows absolutely no sign of slowing down so we can jump off. After being without feedings and water for twelve hours, Adam went into radiology at 4 p.m. While holding Adam on my lap, it was the darndest thing, the tube just started draining.

When the doctor came in, he said, "Whatever you did worked, and I will recommend you in the future." I told him I would send him a bill. After much discussion between the transplant surgeon, the radiologist, and the cardiothoracic people, they have decided to leave his tube in for now, and see how it goes over the weekend. We are relieved Adam did not have to have another procedure, but oh so frustrated this is not clearing up. We are told this is the only thing keeping him in the hospital. Adam was given 140cc of blood today and took a mega nap, so maybe he will be happier this evening. We are now looking at another weekend, with no chance of escape. Since we still have six weeks in Pittsburgh when we get out of here, we may not make our goal of getting home by Thanksgiving. I never thought that was a realistic goal, but Katie is crushed; she really thought that maybe, just maybe.

Day thirty-eight of recovery meant:

It has been forty days and forty nights of living in the hospital. Physical activity still consists of walking the stroller through the halls. Mental activity involves reading newspapers, watching football as Adam allows, and writing to you, on CarePages.

Oh, and talking to the staff about medical stuff, of which I had no interest prior to this. In addition to the time and dose of medication Adam receives, and days of dressing changes, I keep notes on which doctors are due to visit, and big things like which nurse will be on duty each day. I keep the nurses' computer in my room all the time, as it is my only reach to the outside world. Did I say my room?

We spoke to the specialist today about Adam's chest fluid. He is pretty sure it would clear up, if Adam was given more diuretics than he is taking now, but they cannot because of the recent blood clot in his hepatic artery. If they give him more diuretics, it would increase his risk for more clots. So for now, the plan is to wait and see how much drains over the weekend, and discuss it again on Monday. Adam's PICC line was removed today, so one more thing gone.

We are still observing as the nurses do his shots, but one day soon we will have to do it ourselves. We miss our family, church family, and friends so much, but love reading the messages on CarePages, and all the wonderful cards. And on the sports front, U of M beat Illinois, 27-17. Go blue. They have been on a winning streak since I have been locked in here.

Day thirty-nine of recovery was shaping up to be a frustrating one:

Well it's Sunday, and Adam's chest tube is not draining again. Is it clogged or just empty? Transplant has washed their hands of this tube, and turned it over to the cardiac doctors to try and figure out. We noticed the tube was kinked and twisted today, so they had to redo the tape, and dressing around it, and put some little padded board in place to keep it straight. It was a very painful procedure for Adam, and no noticeable fluid began draining. Now we wait for the next x-ray in the morning. If the fluid is not gone, Adam will be facing a new tube, or worse a new procedure to fix the problem. I tried to warn you way back, that I did not want a chest tube, and that it would send me over the edge. Well I am close, so if they do not take it out soon, it will happen for sure. Overall, Adam is starting to smile and laugh a little more, unless you are a doctor, nurse, cleaning person, or anyone that might want to just talk to his parents.

Day forty-one of recovery and with some relief, Joe began:

This morning, Adam's chest x-ray looked very good. We were hoping for removal of the tube today, but the cardiac doc talked to the transplant doc, and all agree the tube is coming out in the morning. Of course what does morning really mean? A doctor will do it before rounds? Or they will round, and a doctor will do it sometime during the day? Anyway, great news, and we must pray it will not be too traumatic, or painful for Adam. Then we watch and see for a day or two what happens. It would be against my protective shell of pessimism to think any positive thoughts, but occasionally a fantasy emerges. I visualize holding Adam's hand, and the two of us walking out of here together.

Day forty-two of recovery was a big day, and Joe wrote:

The day started at 8:30 a.m. with Adam's chest x-ray, in room five on the fourth floor. He handled it very well. Then we waited for transplant to talk to cardiac, and then we waited for rounds, and then we just waited. But it was worth all the waiting, because at 4:45 p.m. our physician's assistant Lisa, removed the tube. Another x-ray tonight just to be sure, and then who knows? He is now free of wires, and enjoys walking the halls with Katie. There are rumors of a possible release for us soon, but I am a little scared. Katie says I "will need special training to re-enter society." I will also have five more kids and a wife again.

Day forty-three of recovery and Joe should not have worried yesterday:

No, I should not have worried yesterday; we are not getting out just yet. Today's x-ray looked good; we are just trying to get the Lovenox levels adjusted. The shots will be restarted tonight, and it looks like I'm up. It will be my first time, so please pray I do not miss and shoot myself. Adam has been very happy and active. He has started talking a lot, and is doing more walking. He enjoys helping his nurse with his vitals, and holds the blue tube for her, when she accesses his mediport. His sleep pattern is a little off but he likes playing, and jumping on my bed until midnight. I'm working on that.

I want to close with this article my aunt sent, which appeared in her church bulletin. It said; I kneel down every night in my room, raise my eyes to Heaven, and pray, and pray, and pray. But nothing ever happens. God does not seem to hear my cry. It goes on to say; someone who felt this way changed his stance, in prayer, and instead of raising his eyes to Heaven, he began to lower his head, and look horizontally when he prayed. What he discovered were the people, and events that filled his everyday life. Suddenly his prayers of petition became less self-centered, and he realized that his own life was so rich with friends, and people who loved him. His give me, give me, give me, prayers were slowly transformed into prayers balanced by heartfelt expressions of praise and thanksgiving, for all God had done for him. Even in the midst of great trial, his prayer became more honest before God. I just want to conclude today by saying this has been our journey, and we pray for all those beautiful people who have been our support.

Chapter 12

Day forty-four of recovery and it looked like this is it:

> They tell us we are free to go except for some prescription snafu. The insurance company, Walgreens, and the doctors are going a few rounds. Technicalities that's all. We are packed; so let's go.

With a hospital wagon trailing behind, Joe made his way from the elevator toward the open lobby with the painted windows. The high sides of the wagon were no match for the accumulation of books, cards, and toys, and Joe stopped often to retrieve a spilled item. Katie pushed Adam in the stroller, which was stuffed with clothes, various medications, and other supplies. A Mickey Mouse balloon was tied to the frame of the stroller. As they entered the lobby, Adam became restless and wanted to walk. Katie gently lifted him out, and he started walking on his own toward the door they had all entered so many weeks ago. About ten feet from the door, Joe called to him, "Adam, wait for me." Gazing tenderly at his son, and taking his hand, Joe fulfilled his fantasy as they walked through the door together. A dark grey foreboding sky, befitting a late October evening, greeted them. The smell of gas fumes, and a definite chill were in the air, and the world never looked so good to Katie and Joe. All at once it hit Joe, he was outside and free to go where he wanted. Well, to some hotel down the street, but still it was the beginning of choices.

With the car loaded, Joe began to wind down the long driveway to Fifth Avenue. Stopping briefly, Joe answered his phone and learned the insurance company would not pay for the Lovenox shots, which were about $1500 a month. They would pay for a generic brand, which Children's Hospital had never used, so figuring out just what dose Adam would need would take a little time. This reinforced the belief that at Adam's first clinic visit next week, they must discuss the possibility of switching him to Coumadin.

Joe pulled into a large alley, behind the hotel, to unload the van. Entering the back door, he saw for the first time where his family had been living this past month. Their suite was the first one inside the back entrance and opened onto the outside balcony walkway. Joe discovered it had a real bed, but asked Katie, "Where is the call button for the nurse?" The grandparents were down the hall, where Katie and Joe had spent their first night in Pittsburgh. Adam had adapted to being one of the kids and obviously enjoyed being able to move around free of cords and IV lines. His siblings were doting on him and maybe carrying him a little too much. Oh well, spending time building up the muscles would begin soon enough.

Late that night, Joe told his readers:

We will stay in the hotel two nights and then move to the home of friends, who have a large finished family room on their lower level. They are relatives of a friend from our church and have very graciously offered to let us stay, for the duration of our time in Pittsburgh. God bless them; I don't know what they are thinking. With the cost of the hotel, I have no idea how we could have managed it, if we were on our own. It's as if the clouds parted and Heaven said, here Joe, one more blessing coming your way.

The next day, Saturday, was pretty much spent packing for the move. Adam had a good day just playing with the other kids and walking frequently from the family's suite down the hall to where the grandmas were. He was adjusting well, but since he only slept in the playpen when they had gone camping, he was pretty sure that's what they must be doing. Katie had some special moments today when Adam asked her to hold him, as he hadn't done that since arriving in Pittsburgh last month. He had been too grouchy, in his constant state of not feeling well, to enjoy any snuggle time.

Joe was doing a great job with Adam's shots. He was giving them away from supervision for the first time, but all went well except the holding down part and tears from his wife. Katie hadn't gotten brave enough to try yet. The hospital gave them an extra four doses of Lovenox, to last until the first clinic visit Monday morning. The insurance company was still refusing to pay, and the generic brand the insurance company wanted the doctors to use was not something the hospital was comfortable giving a child. Given the cost of the shots; this must be worked out. The whole thing was frustrating for Katie and Joe, as his other medicines came through fine and were even delivered to the hotel. The transplant coordinator mentioned admitting Adam to the hospital just to get his Lovenox shots covered by the insurance.

Relating this information to Joe, Katie told him, "I know how ridiculous that sounds and hopefully it will never come to that." Frustrated, Katie added, "I do not understand how they could cover these shots inpatient, but not out. We are cheaper for them if we stay out of the hospital." After Katie updated her readers on life after discharge, she added happy comments from Joe. "Even though I am out of the hospital, U of M is still winning, beating Minnesota 34-10, and I got to watch the game on a big TV."

Sunday morning, for the first time since leaving Michigan, the family attended mass together and gave thanks for their many blessings. There were also prayers for Adam's general health, as he would be on the immunosuppressant drug for maybe a lifetime. Afterwards, the van was packed, the grandma delegation was kissed goodbye, and a short time later the family arrived on the doorsteps of their Pittsburgh hosts. They received a warm welcome and a good meal. The van was unloaded, and the lower level of the house became their new home.

Katie wrote on CarePages late in the day:

Now we prepare for our first clinic visit tomorrow, and hope somehow to get the insurance nightmare straightened out. Joe will take Adam to the appointment because one of us must be here, and if I stay I can keep the school work flowing. We have learned about another miracle going on back home. Neighbors and family members had been working for weeks to plan a benefit pancake breakfast for us. Our church donated the kitchen and hall, and we understand businesses and individuals donated food and door prizes, for the event. We have been told fliers were distributed and information placed in church bulletins in the area. As all these people come together today for the breakfast, we thank the Lord for another incredible blessing. We are blessed with an amazing family, friends, neighbors, church community, and new friends on CarePages. God has been so good to us. Remind me of that the next time I start whining about anything.

On Monday morning Adam awoke to a visiting nurse there to access his mediport and obtain labs for his clinic visit.

After the blood draw, Katie fed Adam quickly and give him his anti-rejection medication. Joe then hurried to the hospital for the 10 a.m. clinic visit, and with traffic and parking, he was only an hour late. After seeing the doctor and being told he had to wait for the lab results, Joe took Adam walking around their old stomping grounds. That's when he remembered, in the rush to get there, he didn't think to raid Katie's purse that morning, For money to pay for hospital parking, and had only four dollars to his name. But he wasn't worried because there was an ATM in the lobby, and he had his bank card with him. Yes, but that is when he remembered it went through the washer last week and did not work. The problem was solved when the information desk gave him the inpatient deal for three dollars a day, making it possible to retrieve his car. Wrapping up his account of the day for Katie, Joe said, "Adam had to have an ultrasound because the labs indicated his liver numbers were slightly elevated, and for old times' sake they also did a chest x-ray, to make sure the chest fluid has not returned. I know Adam was there too long, because he started asking to go back to his room."

The next day the insurance battle rounds came to an end, though not in time for a shipment to arrive for the nightly shot. However, Adam was happy with the news there would be no poke tonight. There were lots of just fun times for him right now; his new best friend was Mickey Mouse, since watching all that Mickey Mouse Clubhouse in the hospital. Watching him on a big TV had been a treat. Adam was almost back to his pre-surgery weight, which was noticeable in his cheeks first, and when the nurse weighed him, he was just a pound under. The Lovenox supply arrived, and the needles were smaller than the ones the hospital sent home. They did not seem quite so intimidating, and Katie gave her first shot.

On Saturday Joe reported to family at home, "The kids had a good Halloween. I sent them out to get me candy, because chocolate helps manage my stress level." Joe and Adam also had another clinic visit yesterday, and the ultrasound was okay for now, but the x-ray showed the pleural effusion had returned. The doctor upped his diuretic from twice a day to three times a day. Unless there was any trouble breathing, they would just wait and see until the next clinic visit on Monday. This started Joe thinking about just what Monday would be like. Adam would start off with the home nurse drawing blood from his mediport. Then I have to rush through Pittsburgh traffic, park the van, drop off the blood, and go to his favorite fourth floor radiology room for a chest x-ray. From there we would go to his clinic visit and if all went well, we would have a genetics doctor appointment at 2 p.m. If the fluid did not go away, the doctor said they would have to put the chest tube back in. We do not want that, Joe thought, as he knew it certainly meant an inpatient procedure. On a day when I am enjoying plenty of football, I must not get ahead of myself with worry. After all, U of M beat Michigan State today, 28-24. Next up is NASCAR, and when it is absolutely necessary, I will start thinking about next week.

Monday morning and Adam was down by ten points with seven minutes to go. His x-ray last week showed fluid, and his liver numbers were up slightly. Well, what do you do? Pray, and pray some more. Sometimes a sports analogy puts things into focus, Joe thought, as he began his busy day. It only took a few minutes into that busy day for Joe to realize he was coming down with a cold, and energy was in short supply. Katie stepped in and said she would take over clinic duties.

Adam woke to face the nurse and another blood draw. Then, having forgotten the anti-rejection drug, his parents tried to give it in the van, after which Adam gagged and threw up. His clothes were changed, and they tried again, this time with success. As Katie left with Adam, she thought about how much she loved being able to go with him to the hospital. Sure, it was nice to get out, but it was great to be involved in his health care and talk to the doctors. Back at home, Joe could be heard to mutter off and on, "Some sick day." He later moaned to Katie, "I had to be teacher and let me tell you, algebra is not my thing. Then there was the laundry, plus, do you know how much stuff there is to constantly pick up? Oh, yeah, I made sure the kids were fed." She listened patiently, and then she updated both Joe and CarePages:

Basically, it seems Adam's chest fluid is gone, and his other lab numbers look good. The liver enzymes went up a little, but the docs do not seem concerned since he had a biopsy two weeks ago, and an ultrasound last week, and both looked good. They have cut back on some meds already, and do not need to see him for a week. We also saw the genetics doctor today, and I expressed concern that Adam has a little trouble walking, and we are worried the disease might be progressing. But I was told it is more likely just because he was bed ridden for so long, and not fully recovered yet.

Katie delighted in telling Joe, "If we want good news from the clinic, I should be the one to take him."

With no clinic visit for a whole week, the family looked forward to living in a low stress environment, but Adam vomited a couple of times and just seemed a little cranky. Katie and Joe believed it must be the current cold bug going around, and it was frustrating for them trying to figure out if and when he was sick and what to do about it. They got very nervous and scared thinking that at any time Adam could be going back to the hospital when he did not feel well. He had been vomiting about once a day, but Katie and Joe believed from all they had learned; it was probably the mitochondrial disease and not liver trouble. He may just have to live with that, as Katie had learned other mitochondrial kids must. There is medication to help with it, but if taken too often, it can lose its effectiveness. He had otherwise been happy and playful, taking long naps during the day, and sleeping through the night. That was also due to the mito disease. The mitochondria were the energy producers, and if they were not producing, the body would run out of energy quickly.

The following Monday, Katie took Adam to the clinic again and came away with good news. Joe started the update saying:

Good evening CarePages family. Katie did a lot of waiting today, but the wait paid off. After seeing Adam, the doctor said there is a good chance we may be home for Thanksgiving. Yes, I said Thanksgiving. Adam's liver numbers look better, and his cold symptoms have pretty much cleared up. Good thing, because my stress level was getting high. I had a break down scheduled for early December, and thought if might be coming early. Well, back to Adam. It looks like the doctor wants to see him next, and if he is not sick, and his numbers look good, he said we could go home.

We are getting credit for time served in the hospital. Forty-six days; I agree that should count for time served. The shots still create anxiety for us, and Adam is going to need therapy to deal with his paranoia when we come near him with anything in our hands.

The whole family went out sightseeing the following week. They went to the Carnegie Science Center and climbed the rock wall, and also took time to explore the city a little. They took a trolley ride, featuring a red car with yellow-framed windows, which took them down Duquesne Incline. The view from the observation deck at the top was breathtaking. As it was early evening when they actually rode down, the lights of the city created a spectacular scene below. The outing was a favorite with the whole family.

Of course Joe also watched football over the weekend and believed it was time to go home, because the winning streak was over for the Wolverines losing first to Wisconsin and next to Ohio State.

Chapter 13

On Monday, Katie once again took Adam to the clinic, and following a very good visit, the doctors decided to cut them loose. Katie wrote on CarePages that evening the very simple, powerful phrase that said it all:

> We're going home! I want to thank our friends on CarePages for the many prayers, uplifting messages, and everyday news from home. Just knowing you were out there following our journey, was a great blessing. I know we will continue to need lots of prayers and support to get through the winter. I will always be waiting for the next time Adam will get sick, or the next time a virus will come into the house. I need prayers to give me peace, and the ability to give everything to God. Another thank you to our hospital angels, who gave so generously of their time, money, and patience. Joe admits special thanks should be given for dealing with him.

That evening as Joe finished loading the van, he reflected on how much fun it had been to tell all the children they were going home. Or as I think back, he remembered, we really didn't have to tell them. Katie came back from the clinic visit with Adam, and one look at her face told them all they needed to hear. Jacob jumped from the couch colliding mid-air with Andy screaming, "Mommy are we going home now?" Katie replied gently, not wanting to squash their hopes, "We can't go yet; we have too much to do first. All of this stuff," she said, with a wave of her arm indicating clothing, toys, and whatever else was strewn around the room, "has to be packed and the car loaded. After that we will all be too tired to do anything but sleep."

With a single pleading voice they spoke an emotional, "Please can we go today?" Joey and Aaron had begun scooping things off the floor, as Joey called out, "Get the box behind the couch and put these game pieces in it, Jackie." Aaron sent an empty Froot Loops box sailing through the air, landing squarely in the waste basket. Katie and Joe looked at each other, and knowing it probably made no sense, told them if they all helped, and promised to sleep in the car, they would somehow do it.

Perhaps it was too much to ask of a family so home sick to wait even another day. Even the youngest children scattered, stuffing crayons into boxes, and packing video games. Soon every corner was searched, the refrigerator emptied; unrecognizable stuff tossed, cupboards were emptied, a load of clothes pulled from the dryer, and all the game pieces rescued and returned to their boxes. So now here they were, stuffing everything they owned into whatever was available and loading it into the van.

Katie and Joe helped the children crawl in among their many possessions, as they made spaces to accommodate the children safely. Adam was tucked into his car seat, and pillows and blankets were finally distributed to everyone. After thanking their hosts profusely, Joe promised to come back soon to pick up the many other things they could not fit into the van.

Everyone slept, at least on and off, and Katie and Joe took turns driving. As he took the all too familiar highway back to Michigan, Joe thought, at least traveling at night with everyone sleeping, we do not have to stop for meals. Adam was the only one who must be fed and Katie managed to do that without having to stop.

At 5 a.m. on the morning of November 20, seventy-one days after leaving their home, eight tired Skorkas pulled into the driveway. What a beautiful sight, went through Joe's mind as he turned off the car. As they stumbled into the house, collapsed for a couple of hours of sleep on various couches and beds, coming home seemed exactly the right thing to do. They woke to boxes, bags, and suitcases littering the living room, with the contents much like a liquid, spilling into every open space. Thus the unpacking began.

Later that morning, while moving a stack of papers pretty much from one place to another, Joe asked Katie about one item in particular. "Where did we get this Make-A-Wish information, and are we doing anything with it?" "Well," Katie replied, "I'm not sure if it was left at the hotel, or sent to us by someone thinking Adam would qualify for the program. I haven't done anything with it because Adam is barely three, and how could he ever express a wish?"

Thanksgiving was celebrated two days later with much more thanks in it this year. Katie wrote a CarePages message two weeks later, hoping everyone had a blessed Thanksgiving:

We were never shy about asking God for what we wanted, and now we must be just as bold about thanking him for all he has given. I remember the words of the man who learned to pray with a different stance, and saw what he had already been given. Same for us; we have family who are always there, friends who are our constant support, and prayers given freely from people we do not know, and will never meet. It is so unbelievably good to be home.

Adam settled quickly into normal home life. One lab came back a little high the first week home and we had a scare, because it turns out the virus he was testing positive for can only be treated at the transplant center in Pittsburgh, and we do not want to go back there. But it was checked again the following week, and had gone down nicely. His liver function is beautiful, and everything else looks good. He will continue to have weekly blood draws for another month or so, and then it will be monthly. Adam still gets his Lovenox shots twice a day, but after next month that should be reduced to once a day. He still hates his immunosuppressant medication, which is also twice a day, because it is sprinkled on his tongue. Anything put in his mouth usually produces a gagging response. He is also getting a little stubborn about it, not opening his mouth, and trying to spit the medicine out. At least he has not been throwing it up. He recovers pretty quickly, and the hope is it will get better with time.

On a morning when labs are drawn, we have to give his Lovenox shot at 4 a.m., because the blood draw needs to be four hours after the shot. But the blood draw also needs to be an hour before his anti-rejection medication, which is given at 9 a.m.

Joe searched daily for work. New housing construction was almost at a standstill, as the entire housing market was slowing down. One day recently he drove ninety-two miles to a job and then came the wind. So he struggled along. A few days before Christmas, Joe made the trip to Pittsburgh to pick up the many things they left behind. The trip meant Katie was alone and nervous about giving Adam his shot and anti-rejection medication. Until now, when she gave them, Joe was there for support. She was relieved to be able to tell him, "I was able to give both the shot and medication while Adam was asleep, and that never happens."

Eager to let everyone know about their Christmas, Katie wrote on CarePages a couple of days later:

Our family had the best Christmas ever. Just being together at home was a blessing, and then we were doubly blessed by so many people who made sure Santa arrived. Many gifts from the Angel Trees lit up the eyes of all the children; but it was Adam who squealed with delight as our home was overrun with all forms of his new special friend, Mickey Mouse. Of course, along with Mickey came Minnie, Pluto, Daisy, Donald, and Goofy. Some of them are large, and he can only carry one, maybe two, at a time. God has turned the suffering and heartache of this past fall into so much good that we don't have the words to explain it. Joe and I were even able to go out alone on our anniversary.

Shortly after Christmas, Katie got the news that a liquid form of Adam's anti-rejection medicine would be tried, because of the difficulty of getting him to take the powder and each dose ending in tears and screaming. The transplant team did not like to do this, because it would bind with the plastic in his g-tube, and the dose would be off. Labs needed to be more frequent in the beginning and, if necessary, his dose would be bumped up to compensate for the loss in the tube. The immunosuppressant level was watched closely, because if it went too high he was vulnerable to any number of viruses in his body that his immune system might not control. His immunity decreased as the level rose. Katie and Joe were advised to avoid large crowds and anyone with symptoms of an illness.

Three large Purell hand sanitizer dispensers were installed in the house; one on the inside wall next to each of the two doors and one in the main floor bathroom. Anyone coming into the house was instructed to use them, and the children and their friends caught on quickly.

With a late Christmas party for extended family looming ahead, Joe's stress level spiked upward. He was worried about ways to keep Adam healthy during these times of contact with other people. Resorting to writing on CarePages, he pleaded, "Please pray the germs away."

By mid-January winter was in full force, and Adam could not go out to play. He asked, but it was just too cold. Joey and Aaron built him an extra large snowman facing the living room window and had him pick out a scarf, hat, and anything else he thought the snowman should wear.

One morning as Adam was watching Mickey Mouse Clubhouse, with his collection of the TV characters surrounding him, Katie asked, "Adam, would you like to see where Mickey Mouse lives and visit his house?" The look on Adam's face was one of total disbelief, and he responded with "Can we go right now?" That was the answer his mother needed. She knew what Adam's wish would be and finally filled out the Make-A-Wish information sheet they had been given.

The clinic in Pittsburgh was very happy with Adam's labs and overall health. They had decided no return trip would be necessary until March. The shots were creating an enormous amount of bruising on his little body, and his legs look like pin cushions, but the anti-rejection medication going into the g-tube had been a blessing. Katie told the family late in January, "We have three more weeks of twice daily shots, and then it is once a day until May. Now we are asking for prayers that he stays healthy this winter and leads a boring uneventful life."

Katie's thoughts now turned to some regular toddler stuff. There was the task of potty training, which up until now had not gone well, and maybe a big boy bed. The plan was always for him to be in Jackie's room on the bottom bunk, but with the feeding pump running all night, Katie couldn't take a chance he might try to get out of bed. He needed to understand the importance of being careful with the tube hooked up, she thought, but maybe over the next year he would be able to move out of our room. He was almost three and a half, but he still seemed like a baby with diapers, a crib, and formula. But as she told Joe, "He is so smart; I think he will be doing his own tube feedings before long."

On February 4, the Lovenox shots were cut down to once a day. It was a day of wishing Adam could understand there would be no more evening pokes, and also hoping that his legs would start healing and that soon the bruising would disappear. Katie updated CarePages with other news:

Adam's diuretic was discontinued, so his diaper shouldn't be quite as soaked in the morning. We are now down to eight medications, but some of those are vitamins that he will be on forever. We will be going back to Pittsburgh next month, but I am a little reluctant to set up the appointment. I am afraid they will want to schedule his last surgery. Adam's muscles, at the top of his incision, were left open to accommodate the growing liver. Sometimes the muscles close on their own, but if not it must be done in surgery. Adam also has a stitch that is coming through near his incision site and seems to be causing a little discomfort. It will have to be trimmed, or something awful like that. It's actually from the stitches on the inside, but one has started to poke up through the skin. Adam shows no interest in eating, but he has discovered chocolate. He will ask for a piece, and just suck on it. He won't use his teeth, or try to get a big part in his mouth, but he obviously enjoys the taste.

In February, a cold virus swept into the house beginning with Adam, and soon the whole family was coughing and sneezing. At least it took away the fear of passing it on to Adam. Katie had things pretty well handled until Joe showed the same symptoms. Then she was heard to say, "Somehow he is sicker than the kid on the immunosuppressant drugs. He is also a more difficult patient."

Blood was drawn to monitor Adam's levels during this time. A few days later the results of one of the labs showed the Epstein Barr virus level was high. The transplant center kept a close eye on it, because it was only treatable by lowering the immunosuppressant drug, so his body could fight off the virus. The higher EBV number may be due to his cold, but it also may be his body saying it is time to lower his immunosuppressant. The medication dose was decreased to see how his body responded. The down side was that weekly blood draws were needed until it all stabilized.

Adam had started asking the other kids where their liver was. He had noticed they did not have a lovely scar across their abdomens, and he thought the scar was called your liver. Katie enjoyed sharing this story with others, especially the response Andy gave when asked that question. He simply replied, "I don't have a liver, Adam."

Answering the phone one snowy day late in February when the thermometer outside read 15 degrees, Katie found herself speaking to a Make-A-Wish representative. Adam had qualified for a wish, and she would be coming to the house next week to explain the process. They were not only going to make Adam's wish come true, but provide a much deserved reward for the other children, who had willingly sacrificed so much time with their parents for the sake of their little brother. Wanting to learn more about the organization, Katie discovered the foundation began in 1980, when a little boy with a life threatening medical condition realized his wish of becoming a police officer. Since then the organization had reached more than 174,000 children around the world. Volunteers served as wish granters, special event assistants, and generously gave of their time wherever they were needed. The foundation relied on donations of time and money from individuals and corporations to continue this work.

The process of granting a wish consisted of four steps. The first was to obtain a referral. This could come from the medical community, parents, family, and even the affected child. Children must be at least two and a half years of age and under the age of eighteen at the time of referral. The second step was to determine a child's medical eligibility. The treating physician was consulted, and the diagnosis must reflect a life threatening medical issue, such as a progressive, degenerative, or malignant condition.

The third step was to send a wish team to learn about the child's special wish. They searched for the one experience that would delight that child. The fourth step was to create the unforgettable experience that would enrich the child and the family with hope, strength, and joy, giving them something positive to look forward to, and even a belief in the future, when there wasn't a cure. Now, they were about to do the same thing for Adam and his family.

The following week the representative had some very happy news. She said, "You are all going to Florida and spend five days at Disney World sometime in the spring."

During a conversation with the transplant coordinator, Katie learned their Pittsburgh visit could wait until after Easter. Adam would be over his six-month transplant anniversary, she thought, so he must be doing really well in their eyes too. Although his immunity level had not decreased much yet, the transplant team thought it might take another week of the lower dosed med before it reflected in the labs. They were surprised at how great Adam's magnesium and potassium levels looked. Relating this on CarePages Katie said:

> Transplant kids often have trouble with these levels. In fact, the coordinator thought he was on medication to regulate them, but he is not. Adam has used the potty several times; it sort of depends on his mood, but at least he is trying. We are so proud of what a wonderful kid he is with all he has been through. Even all the spoiling we have done hasn't turned him into a monster. He is so polite and enjoyable.

The first week of March brought another scare, and Katie wrote on CarePages:

> Adam developed a slight fever today, and of course fevers can be a sign of liver rejection. But it could just be from his cold. His immunosuppressant is the lowest it has been. The last lab put it at 4.2, and the transplant team likes it between 6 and 10. Why do these things always happen on the weekends, when the only way to get a medical question answered is to call an emergency number? We are not supposed to give him Tylenol until we talk to them, and they said to only call if the fever is 101, and his is 100.2. Hopefully it will not creep up overnight. He is having a hard time sleeping with this cough, and so he is a little crabby.

But Katie knew whether or not Adam was able to get some sleep tonight, she would not.

The next evening, Joe went back to the computer and updated CarePages as he had so often.

> Adam's fever climbed to 102.2 today, so we called and got the okay for Tylenol. His cold is worse, and I am starting to have flash backs of him being miserable and crabby, and those long nights in the hospital. I know it's just a cold, but it's frustrating when I can't help him. I thought I might talk to my old friends, and ask for a few prayers to just help Adam and his brother Aaron, who is miserable along with him, get over these colds. Adam is still watching a lot of Mickey Mouse Clubhouse, just like the hospital days, and I hope he will go to sleep before

midnight. And one more thing; sorry to be whining, I certainly know it could be a lot worse.

Within three days Adam was feeling much better and had his first neurology appointment since the transplant. It was at this point, Katie remembered that everything had been revolving around transplant related stuff, and not much attention had been given to his mitochondrial disease. The doctor, having seen Adam's biopsy reports for the first time, said, "I want to do an MRI of his brain." "Why, since Adam isn't showing signs of the disease progressing?" Katie asked. Driving home, she acknowledged that his answer made sense of "Wanting to keep tabs on it." It's just that the transplant had been so successful, and she and Joe had gotten used to g-tube feedings and the mito cocktail full of vitamins. The suggestion that there may be more trouble down the road was a difficult one to take in. The neurologist did agree that Adam was doing well developmentally.

In March, another request for prayers went out. The transplant clinic called and reported Adam's white blood count was too low. It had been creeping downward for several weeks, but his ANC stayed above 1,000, so it was considered in the acceptable range. But now the ANC was around 700, and the white count was down even more. The ANC, or absolute neutrophil count, was the number of white blood cells that are neutrophils and fight infection. Neutrophils make up about 55 to 70 percent of total white blood cells. A low ANC translates into a high risk for infection, and at this point meant Adam had very little ability to fight off infections and bacteria. Coupled with the cough he seemed unable to shake, the transplant clinic wanted Adam to be seen by his pediatrician, who would listen to his lungs, and if he heard anything suspicious, would order a chest x-ray. Thoughts of how nervous Adam gets about little rooms and not knowing if something was going to hurt or not, preoccupied

Katie as she drove to the doctor's office. She also realized his body couldn't fight this virus on its own, so it was important to ask for prayers to help him.

By mid-afternoon Adam had been seen by the pediatrician, and Katie was able to report that he was very compliant, taking deep breaths and opening his mouth when asked. The results were good, as his lungs were clear and his ears showed no sign of infection. Katie told her family, "We will be keeping him home, until we get permission to take him out in public again." She added, "Poor kid, he has been home so much he actually thinks a trip to the doctor is fun."

The next day Adam's EBV numbers had more than doubled, so the transplant clinic cut his medication again. They believed his body was trying to say it was over suppressed, and that is why the colds had been so bad and the EBV climbed. With the very low white blood count of 2.1, Adam would need two injections a day of Nupogen, which would stimulate the bone marrow to produce more white blood cells. Katie had been advised that the shots were more painful than the Lovenox shots he was currently getting. Her response on CarePages was:

> It could be a rough few days, as the Nupogen can also cause bone pain. It is scary to know his immune system is so off during this time of year. Labs have been ordered for Monday and hopefully the results will be available early in the week. We count on your prayer support on these days when we worry so much.

Adam handled his Neupogen injections well, and they didn't seem to bother him anymore than the Lovenox shots did. The next set of labs showed his white count up; so the third Neupogen injection was cancelled. Follow-up labs would indicate how his liver was handling all this, and the hope was that the lower dose of immunosuppressant medication would allow his body to fight off the EBV.

The labs did indeed show the EBV level had dropped dramatically, and the lower dose of medication proved to be enough. His liver was handling this beautifully.

Feeding therapy was at the heart of the conversation with the gastroenterologist during a recent visit. There had been a very brief attempt, when Adam was about a year old, but he hated the three times a week sessions of playing with food. He had been encouraged to touch the food, and push it around on the high chair tray; and the idea of food being your friend was promoted. A lot of screaming followed when something was actually put in his mouth. After his tests began to show how sick Adam was, feeding therapy was abandoned. Now, the idea of starting it again was very unpleasant, but the doctor told Katie, "It's all up to you, and what you think Adam can handle right now." She left the office filled with doubt, as conflicting thoughts went through her mind. There was no proof that Adam's feeding issues were from the mitochondrial disease, but at this point it felt like they must be. Wasn't he too young when all of this started for it to be a psychological thing? It had been three years, so you'd think we would see improvement not deterioration, over that time, she rationalized. The therapy sessions before were so stressful. If there was only a way to find out for sure about the mito in his GI tract, but no one seemed to think there was. Katie settled the issue in her mind, by deciding to bring it up in June during their visit to the geneticist. Right now all her concentration must be on the brain scan scheduled for this week.

Later on CarePages, she asked for prayers:

We are praying that the results will show no neurological progression of the mito disease. We are also asking for prayers for Joe, as he looks for work. Life has been stressful enough, and this extra burden has been quite a handful. We know God will provide; it would just be nice to know His plan a little in advance.

April 1 came and Adam's MRI went well. Now they waited for the results. The transplant clinic called with some good news the same day, saying Adam's liver function numbers were very good, with the lower dose of anti-rejection medication. "No more pokes Adam," Katie said, feeling a great sense of relief, when told the Lovenox shots were also to be discontinued.

During the same conversation, an appointment was scheduled for Adam to be seen in mid-April. Katie was told a donor appreciation dinner was scheduled for that weekend in Pittsburgh, and she and Joe began looking forward to seeing some of the other transplant families.

A week later the MRI results showed that all looked normal and this scan would be used as a baseline for any future MRIs. Katie reported on CarePages:

Adam surprised everyone by taking a few bites of yogurt today. Once in a while he will take a bite or two of something and not do it again, but this time he had several bites and even fed himself. This is a very good sign, and hopefully he will continue to take these baby steps. On another happy note we heard from Make-A-Wish, and our trip to Disney World is scheduled for the first week of June.

Adam was very excited that he is finally going to meet Mickey Mouse and visit his home.

Adam began asking on a daily basis, "How much longer until I go to Mickey's house?" This trip was a dream come true for all the children, Katie thought. There was no way Joe and I could ever afford to take them on any trip, let alone to Disney World. They all went through the difficult times of having their parents away, living in a hotel for a couple of months, and just generally having their lives turned upside down. This was a great reward for doing all that with such love and compassion for their little brother, with rarely a complaint.

The following week Katie, Joe, and Adam made the familiar trip to Pittsburgh. The donor appreciation dinner was a nice chance to visit and to compare notes with other transplant families. The donors received medals, and those who had gone through so much as recipients were recognized. Dr. Mazariegos and the other transplant team doctors were there, so families took advantage of the opportunity to take pictures with their surgeon.

Katie wrote after the clinic visit:

We had a 10:30 a.m. appointment, but were not seen until 1:30 p.m. It reminded us of our days in the hospital, and trying to keep Adam amused for any length of time. But it was a good visit and the surgeon said Adam is doing very well, and he is not recommending any changes for now. A stitch protruding from the incision site still bothers him at times, and will be taken care of when we come back to see the genetics doctor in June. It will be an outpatient treatment, requiring a little sedation. We will not need to see the transplant people for a year, unless of course there is trouble.

School had been a little off schedule for Katie and the kids this year. They did as much as possible while in Pittsburgh, but it certainly was not the schedule they would have followed at home. But now Katie realized, with the Disney World trip scheduled for June, everyone had been working very hard, and it was a great motivator toward trying to get the school year completed before the trip.

May arrived and the promise of spring, in the form of trees whose buds seemingly opened overnight, the sun that warmed the earth, bursts of sunshine colored yellow daffodils, and an array of colorful tulip blooms. May also featured the first communicants freshly scrubbed in beautiful new clothes. Family and friends gathered at mass to celebrate seven-year old Jacob's First Communion, and to thank the Lord for another blessing.

The countdown was now twenty days to seeing Mickey. The lab results were the best they had ever been, and Adam was on the lowest dose possible of his anti-rejection medicine. The phone call, with the lab results, put to rest fears of doing the muscle closing surgery in June. When the surgeon said Adam needed to grow a little first, Katie and Joe didn't realize that meant two to three years. Somehow the idea it had to be done within the first year after the transplant took hold and grew, causing much worry. Now a sense of relief set in knowing the surgery would be put off until he reached school age.

The weather was perfect for Adam. It had not turned hot yet and he could be outside, without wilting from the heat. As Katie followed the Florida weather, however, she knew the temperature there was in the 90s. On the recommendation of other mito families, a cooling vest had been ordered. It should regulate his temperature nicely and last most of the day.

A few days before the Florida trip, two representatives from the Make-A-Wish Foundation came to the house bearing balloons and tubs of chocolate, vanilla, and strawberry swirl ice cream. The ice cream was covered with chocolate fudge, butterscotch, caramel, marshmallow, and strawberry sauces. Toppings of bananas, chopped peanuts, sprinkles, chopped candy bars, maraschino cherries, and crushed chocolate cookies were sprinkled on top. Lots of whipped cream covered everything. As everyone ate, Adam amused himself by playing with the cans of whipped cream. Pulling Adam on his lap, Joey offered him a bite of ice cream; but Adam simply sprayed another large dollop of whipped cream in Joey's bowl. Gifts were given, including sunglasses and white tee shirts emblazoned with Make-A-Wish for the family to wear, if desired, on the plane as well as in the park. Lots of pictures were taken during the evening, and Katie thought about how festive it all was as her head hit the pillow that night. As if the kids needed anything else to get them excited for the trip. These people have been wonderful to us, and have made us believe that for a short time we really will live in the land of Disney. Now if I could only sedate Joe before his day of flying with six kids, she thought, as she drifted off to sleep.

Chapter 14

The Florida days were filled with magic and fun, as the Make-A-Wish people provided a dream vacation which was way beyond anyone's imagination. Not only were there visits to Disney World and endless rides, but the family stayed in a place called Give Kids the World Village, which in itself was an incredible experience.

Walt Disney World's favorite characters visited the village providing one on one time with the children and opportunities for keepsake photographs. Adam and all the children had incredible days of meeting Mickey, Minnie, Goofy, Pluto, and even Barney. One morning Mickey and Minnie visited the village; another morning it was Barney and friends. Adam was shy at first, but came around pretty quickly when he got his first big hug from Mickey. Where else could a child go and get a hug from these special characters? Katie and Joe agreed the picture of Adam sitting on Mickey's lap was priceless.

The family visited Mickey's house, and Adam was particularly interested in his bed and refrigerator. Katie and Joe reported home saying, "We can't praise the volunteers and employees at the village enough." The volunteers even fixed problems above and beyond the expected. Katie had shipped Adam's formula ahead to arrive the day they did, because thirty-six cans would be too much to carry with them. The package was lost in shipping, but the village was able to get enough of the same formula to get him through the week.

The wonderful story of the village began with a little girl named Amy, who was very ill and wanted to come to Florida. A request of a complimentary stay was made of a respected hotelier. He was glad to oblige, as he had done so often in the past. Travel plans took too long to arrange, however, and Amy passed away before her wish could be granted. The hotelier's name was Henri Landwirth, and he made a vow that no child in need would ever be failed again, and this story would never repeat itself. Mr. Landwirth enlisted aid from colleagues in the hotel business and the area theme parks to bring these special children and their families to central Florida, in as little as twenty-four hours if necessary. He called the project Give Kids the World because that is just what he intended to do. He planned to provide a magical cost-free experience for children with life threatening illnesses and their families. Children with a daily regimen of medicine, needles, and treatments, would come here and find laughter, and a lifetime of memories. No child in need has ever been turned away, and no child ever will be, it is the promise Give Kids the World lives by.

As the number of families visiting the village continued to grow, more space was necessary and the seventy-acre resort village opened in 1989. Individuals generously contributed money. Corporations and wish granting organizations also came together to welcome families from all fifty states and more than sixty-five countries.

The village provides three day park hopper tickets to Walt Disney World for the families staying in one of the more than one hundred villas. In addition, it offers a dream vacation within its perimeter. Families are met at the airport by their personal greeter, there to assist with luggage and coordinating transportation. A rental car is supplied by Make-a-Wish and is made available for the duration of the trip.

Inside the village is a carousel, housed under a large red mushroom, offering endless rides outside the Castle of Miracles. Inside the castle a star was hung from the ceiling for each wish child who visits. The star will remain forever.

Meals served in the Gingerbread House are compliments of Perkins Family Restaurant, which began providing meals soon after the village opened. The restaurant looked like something out of a storybook, with candy cane pillars, and characters popping out of upstairs windows. An ice cream parlor, open all day, provided unlimited goodies to stretch the imagination, and create a gooey fantasy. Precious smiles are the end result. As with meals, ice cream is complimentary. Outside, a life size board game begins with children taking the part of the moving characters in a game of Candy Land. A wonderful pool keeps everyone comfortable in the Florida sun.

Disney World cast members also volunteer to serve meals, scoop ice cream, greet families at the airport, and entertain through shows at the village. Through the combination of Disney World and Give Kids the World Village, children are given the chance to wish upon a star and have their dreams come true.

On the way home, the flight out of Orlando was delayed five times, and finally after a wait of six hours, the flight was cancelled. Make-A-Wish got the family a hotel room nearby and arranged for the village to send a volunteer with more formula. There was enough to get through the night and the next day's flight home. Katie commented after the trip, "These volunteers and the village employees were such a blessing. We truly did live in the land of Disney for a short time."

Chapter 15

Several weeks later, Katie, Joe, and Adam were back in Pittsburgh for the much anticipated visit with Dr. Vockley, as well as to have the protruding stitches taken care of. Katie told family, "Adam seems excited about the trip, and asked if he could see the hospital, and the purple elevators. We are hoping his enthusiasm lasts throughout the trip."

Once in Pittsburgh, Adam's stitches were removed without an overnight stay, and they were on their way to the genetics appointment. It was a good visit; a lot of time was spent answering Katie and Joe's questions. Relaying what they learned to family, Katie said, "Dr. Vockley was very open about Adam's prognosis. One thing he was clear about, 'Adam is a bona fide miracle.' Those were Dr. Vockley's words, and he also said, 'Adam will be my poster child' for pushing the transplant committee into agreeing to let other children with mitochondrial disease qualify for transplant."

In response to what she had been told, Katie said she "was mad at God" ten months ago for not giving us a miracle and healing Adam's liver; but "now I see what a miracle the surgery was." Dr. Vockley also said during the visit, "Looking at the biopsy results from Adam's muscle tissue; I would expect a kid with those numbers to be doing much worse." As good as this is, he still expects to see some progression of the disease, but cannot guess when, since many other kids with similar symptoms; severe liver failure, and minor muscle symptoms, did not survive the liver failure.

Katie and Joe felt humbled knowing Adam may help other kids get more help with transplant options. Dr. Vockley planned to write a paper chronicling Adam's progress and his response to the transplant. There was a concern that the surgery would cause a crisis in Adam's body, and the mito might get worse, but that had not happened. Using leftover tissue from his pre-transplant biopsy, gene testing would begin to see if the gene causing the mito disease could be isolated. It is unclear how long it will take to get results, and Katie and Joe were warned the chances are slim that the gene could be isolated. The fragility of this disease, and the reality that symptoms indicating its progression could appear at any time, was something they would have to live with.

While asking for continuing prayers on CarePages, Katie voiced a special thank you.

> Even the doctors admit Adam's miracle status, and we know it is due to our prayer warriors. We thank God for Dr. Vockley as well, for fighting for Adam, and helping save his life.

It was mid-July when the call came from the genetics counselor. Baylor University had identified the mutated gene. Katie organized her thoughts and presented the new information on CarePages:

> The gene is the Mpv 17, and is found in the protein membrane of the mitochondria. Adam has two bad copies, one from each parent, which caused the disease. Baylor also wants more liver or muscle tissue, from previous biopsies, to do a copy number analysis. This basically means delving more deeply into the data derived from a test on DNA a child receives from both parents. It was a surprise to have the results back so quickly, but since it was an already identified mutated gene, it popped up in their

first round of tests. This mutation has only been identified since 2006, and since it has only been a couple of years, not many other kids have been diagnosed yet. This means not much is known about a prognosis for Adam's future. As the genetics doctor said before, not many other children survived the liver disease stage of this.

Blood tests will need to be done on Katie and Joe to confirm they each gave Adam a copy of the mutation. It will be up to them whether or not to have the other children tested, with a simple blood test. Katie and Joe were comforted by the fact that everyone with this mutated gene, has presented in infancy like Adam, with liver disease as the main symptom. So the probability of their other children having it was slim, as they have no symptoms and are considerably older now. The genetics counselor told Katie, "There isn't much information available on this mutation because it is so new. For the most part, Adam will be the example others down the road will look to for a prognosis." She did say, "The few other children that received a liver transplant were also currently doing well." This was from information she received at a recent mito conference.

Mulling all this over after she spoke to the counselor, Katie's feelings were that as nice as it is to have a firm reason for his disease, this genetics stuff is very confusing. But God has taken good care of Adam for these almost four years, and we know He will keep him covered in the future.

Two weeks later Katie updated CarePages with:

Adam's monthly labs came back very good again. He likes to help the nurse, and hold the tubes for her. When she is finished, he always thanks her. He is definitely back to his polite and charming ways. Adam has been feeling great and is enjoying summer. He loves to play outdoors, but must spend the hottest part of the day inside. We were able to take him for his first trip to Michigan's Adventure Amusement Park this week. On the last day in Florida, Give Kids the World Village gave us a list of amusement parks that we could get free passes to, once each, for one year. Michigan's Adventure was on the list, and the whole family was able to go. Adam loved it. He wore his cooling vest and enjoyed so many rides for the first time. He has no fear of anything, and I am sure he would have gone on the roller coaster if he was tall enough. The water part of the park was perfect for him, with the cooling effect, and he wanted to try everything. As Joe and I watched him play, we realized how different it is this summer having him so healthy and happy.

A cardiologist appointment late in August intruded on the wonderful summer. It was very hard on Adam, as he hates the stickers for the EKG so much, and even now remembers that he had eighteen of them. He did well for the ultrasound though, and everything related to his heart is perfect.

At the end of August, Adam's labs looked good and his aspirin regimen was discontinued. He had been taking aspirin since he left the hospital, and now he was finished with all blood thinners. Hopefully, this would mean an end to his frequent bruising. As far as daily medications, he was still taking his anti-rejection medication, an antibiotic, four vitamins, and a drug he now took to regulate his potassium level. "I have noticed," Katie told family members, "He has been falling a little more often lately. I think it is usually noticeable the day after an especially busy day, when he has been very active. I will start paying more attention to that, but it would make sense. He doesn't seem to be hurting, but some days there does seem to be a little weakness in his legs."

Adam is happy and potty trained, except for nighttime, and loves to stir peanut butter in the jar, and once in a while decides to take a bite.

Chapter 16

On September 12, an emotional message was placed on CarePages:

> Today we fall on our knees and thank God, for letting us keep Adam. It's hard to believe it has been an entire year since his liver transplant. When I think about our mindset last year at this time; it's overwhelming how far we've come. It's embarrassing to think about how I questioned God, and worried so much. I still worry about Adam, but if God can pull us through last fall, we can get through anything. I also think of what the other kids had to go through, and feel so proud of them, and the way they handled it, and are still handling everything.

> We are so blessed, and I hope I don't ever get to a place again where I forget that, or doubt God's providence. He has taken Adam on such a journey toward better health. His liver continues to do well and he's been healthy. His mito symptoms still seem to be only that he's not as sure on his feet as other kids his age. He has some muscle weakness, but that kid sure makes up for it with his determination. He loves to climb and run and jump. I don't know how those skinny little legs can take him anywhere, but he tries so hard to keep up with all the other little kids running around the neighborhood. He falls often, but never stops trying.

The neurologist said when he falls; he falls forward more like tripping instead of his legs giving out on him. And of course he is still tube fed, but enjoys occasional drinks and some bites of food. We haven't given up on that. Most important we want to thank our prayer warriors who continue to remember Adam, and all the people that helped us in Pittsburgh, and back home. We love you all.

As Katie concluded her update on this special day, Joe had a surprise of his own prepared. To each of his hospital angels, helpers, and Katie, he presented an angel pin, accented with the recipient's birthstone.

Two days later, Adam celebrated his fourth birthday surrounded by a loving family. "Any birthday outside of a hospital is a good one," Katie said, as she prepared to light the candles on his Mickey Mouse cake. "And Adam has grown a little more than five inches, and gained about four pounds this past year. Amazing what a new liver can do for you." She went on to tell the family gathered for this happy occasion, "His bruising has subsided a lot, and now his skin looks more normal. We haven't had the heart, or courage, to take away his binky yet. We wanted to when he turned four, but we've spoiled him, and have to work on that."

Adam received all the vaccines a child is supposed to during his first two years. However, he cannot get the booster shots for the ones that are live viruses, including chicken pox, because of the medication that lowers his immunity.

One Sunday, Adam insisted on sitting with his little friend in church, who has since been diagnosed with a mild case of chicken pox. Katie wasn't worried about it, but called the transplant team just to run it by them. Their response startled her. They ordered immediate blood work, to see if he's infected. Since it takes five days for results, and they don't want to wait, they started Adam on

Acyclovir, in hopes of keeping it at bay. If it does break out, he needs to be admitted to the hospital to receive anti-viral medicine, through an IV for a week. It's tricky because they would have to lower his anti-rejection medication to fight the virus and watch closely for any liver rejection. If that happened, he would have to be admitted to the hospital in Pittsburgh. The hardest part was waiting the three-week incubation period to see if he was in the clear or not. Some children, who have gotten the vaccine, get such a mild case of the disease it may not be recognized. Since Adam cannot get the booster, his parents know they will always have to be on the lookout.

Once again, things have a brighter outcome than expected. Adam's lab results showed he was immune to chicken pox. The thinking was that his first vaccine got a boost when he received Katie's liver, because she had chicken pox as a child. The doctors would continue to study this possibility, but Katie didn't care how it happened; it was one less thing to worry about. "And we thank God," Katie said, as she gave the news to Joe, "for the amazing way He continues to take care of Adam."

A few weeks later, at a follow-up genetics visit in Pittsburgh, Katie and Joe received some much anticipated information. It was explained to them, that Adam's disease was inherited in an autosomal recessive manner, with both parents being unaffected carriers. Adam inherited one-gene depletion on a chromosome from Katie and a different type of depletion from Joe.

Each of their children had a 25 percent chance of getting it. Each child also had a 25 percent chance of not getting it at all, and a 50 percent chance of being a carrier like their parents.

The problem was this particular gene depletion on the chromosome, within the DNA, had only been identified within the last two years, and there was really no information on it yet. The other kids that have been found with this gene depletion all present the same way, with early liver failure and skeletal muscle involvement. The good news is that so far none of them have any neurological impairment. The kids that had the liver disease corrected through a liver transplant have been doing well. They were also able to run a brand new test on Adam's old liver and muscle tissue that revealed how much of his mitochondria in those areas were functioning properly. The old liver had only 19 percent and that explains the rapid liver failure. The muscle shows 78 percent of his mitochondria as functioning well. So the low energy levels were to be expected. The doctor did say Adam's 78 percent number is higher than any of the other patients in the testing pool. Granted, there haven't been many children tested yet, but it is good news. With this fairly high number, the doctor doesn't expect a very rapid progression in his muscles, but he has nothing to base this prognosis on other than how well Adam is doing. Katie and Joe were given permission not to worry about Adam's lack of eating, because he felt it would most likely happen on its own. It will probably take several years, and it is important not to stress the energy cells, or mitochondria, by letting him get too hungry, or he could get worse. He needs enough calories to grow properly. He will also need yearly evaluations by a cardiologist, a neurologist, and the ophthalmologist, to check these high-energy organs that could become involved. Since the level of functioning mitochondria in his heart, brain, and eyes cannot be checked, he will need to be watched for symptoms.

After explaining these long awaited findings on CarePages that night, Katie closed by saying;

We pray for a healthy future for Adam, and for all our CarePages families. Thank you for checking on him, as he struggles with this frustrating disease, and remembering him in your prayers; as we also remember the many other children also affected by mitochondrial disease.

The next year passed quickly. Adam's labs were consistently good and giving the immunosuppressant, Prograf, through his g-tube continued to be a blessing. The year 2008 would be the first year of Adam's life with no hospitalizations.

Early in 2009, with labs still very good, Adam's overnight formula drip would be discontinued and those calories added to his daytime feedings. The yearly EKG and echocardiogram, to check mitochondrial disease effects on the heart, were good.

When Adam complained of leg pain at night his Carnitine, an amino acid, dose was doubled to help with that discomfort. As he blew out five candles on his cake in September, Katie and Joe noted that each birthday is a happy celebration of life.

Adam's yearly transplant clinic visit, in November 2009, would be at the new Children's Hospital. The doctors were very happy with his progress and the geneticist reminded Katie and Joe this is uncharted water as many other patients, with his form of mito disease, did not survive the liver failure. He was once again called the poster child for getting other mito kids help with liver transplants. With labs consistently good, the doctor decreased his dose of Prograf.

Although monthly labs looked good, in March 2010, Adam was often lethargic and complained of leg pain. The usual checks for virus and infection were negative. Soon abdominal pain, fever, and the complaint of consistently feeling hot would lead to evaluation in the emergency room. An ultrasound showed two large masses in Adam's abdomen and a CT scan showed masses on the kidneys, enlarged lymph nodes, and possible nodules on his liver. The transplant team wanted Adam transferred to Pittsburgh immediately and he and Katie would be airlifted during the night arriving at 4:30 a.m. The small plane could accommodate one parent leaving Joe to drive through the night arriving later that morning. The surgeon explained the masses would most likely be lymphoma and there are three types and three different ways to treat them. It is probably caused by the high level of EBV in his body; the Epstein-Barr virus that most people have in their system but must be monitored closely in transplant patients because it's hard for them to keep it at bay. It is checked every three months and labs were due this month. Adam's last level was 10,000, and when drawn with other labs on arrival at Children's Hospital, was 430,000. Prograf would be stopped.

A spinal tap and biopsies of the bone marrow and liver would reveal Burkitt's type PTLD and with Burkitt in the bone marrow it is leukemia. Post Transplant Lymphoprolifertive Disorder (PTLD) is a rare complication affecting only two percent of transplant kids. PTLD which turns out to be Burkitt's type is even more rare. For PTLD-Burkitt's to be leukemia has been reported fewer than five times the doctor believes. Then for the rare PTLD Burkitt's leukemia to be in a mitochondrial patient is unique. The oncology expert consulted with other experts all over the world and no cases had been documented. Once again Adam was in uncharted territory. Chemo would begin and had already been injected during the spinal tap, because that's a hard area to diagnose, and it would be better to give the chemo to be safe. Adam would be moved to the oncology floor and the transplant team and genetics would continue to follow him.

Katie and Joe felt overwhelmed by fear and frustration seeing Adam frightened and in pain; they also felt they had run away from home in the middle of the night without being able to explain the situation to their five children at home. Katie updated information on CarePages several times a day; each time asking readers to pray for a miracle.

The oncologist said the leukemia was the fastest growing type in humans and highly aggressive; Adam probably did not have it in his body two months ago. Treatment would be aggressive but could not be as aggressive as for a non-transplant patient, let alone one with mitochondrial disease. It would be a difficult balance. Chemo would be given for seven days and then progress would be evaluated. An MRI showed no nervous system involvement with the Burkitts.

In addition to chemo, Adam would be on prednisone and a series of drugs that would work with the chemo. He developed painful mouth sores and a sore throat in response to the treatment.

A week later Joe went home to bring their other five children and Grandma to Pittsburgh for a week. They would stay with the same friends who welcomed the family after transplant and would be able to spend time with Adam. The children raised Adam's spirits getting him to talk and smile. Jacob brought action figures and spent hours on Adam's bed playing with him while Joey blew into the nurses' latex gloves filling the room with an assortment of balloon animals.

After several days an MRI was done and the mass in the abdomen had decreased in size. A bone marrow biopsy showed no cancer cells remained. The treatment was working.

Another side effect for Adam was unexplained tummy pain. He also dealt with severe nerve pain primarily in his feet from the drugs given with the chemo. Most nights Katie sat at his bedside while he held her hand and she rubbed his feet. As Joe drove the children and Grandma back to Michigan, Katie prayed for wisdom for the doctors and for the miracle that would heal Adam.

Another week of chemo began and a few days later an MRI would show all masses on the liver, kidney, and in the abdomen were gone. Adam would need blood transfusions during treatment, very common in chemo kids. With Adam's ANC numbers close to zero a mask would be required when he left the room.

The doctors at Children's Hospital began coordinating with oncology doctors in Grand Rapids as Adam would still need five months of chemo; since all tests were clear, they felt it could be done at home. Adam's hair was falling out in small clumps and, once home, Katie buzzed it. Having been on TPN or IV nutrition while in Pittsburgh, Adam would remain on that at home for now.

A week later chemo began with one overnight stay followed a few days later by a fever and diagnosis of a staph infection in his port and bloodstream. IV antibiotics would be started in the hospital and would be completed at home using his port.

Adam enjoyed camping during the summer and in September was blessed with a puppy from a local cancer charity; the whole family welcomed him.

The chemo series continued; some inpatient and several done at home until completion of the five month series. A bone marrow biopsy would be done two weeks later and a CT scan done three weeks after completion. In the beginning, follow-up scans would be done every other month for six months and then every three months for at least a year. At that time a new schedule would be adopted as scans would be necessary for several more years.

During a visit to genetics, it was decided a powder containing extra calories would be added to Adam's formula to compensate for the weight lost during treatment. The immunosuppressant drug would be discontinued permanently with frequent labs to watch for signs of liver rejection. Adam would be part of a research study on why some kids need immunosuppressant medicine and some don't.

By spring of 2011 physical therapy would be started to strengthen the muscles in his legs; Adam enjoyed going to his own gym and working out. He had gained 10 pounds since the cancer diagnosis and finished kindergarten on time in spite of chemo. Now in the summer of 2012 he has completed first grade and made his First Communion.

The labs have all been excellent and show the liver is handling the lack of immunosuppressant beautifully. Adam's meds now consist of vitamins and carnitine. There is still the challenge of food. Adam doesn't eat except for an occasional bite of something and six chocolate chips when a friend or sibling is having a snack. Although some muscle weakness exists in Adam's legs, he keeps up with the other kids and never ever stops trying.

While celebrating the fifth anniversary of Adam's liver transplant, Katie and Joe are so grateful to Dr. Vockley who fought for the transplant; thus paving the way for allowing other mitochondrial kids the same opportunity. His parents admit they will always worry as a scan date approaches or whether some little ache or pain is the cancer returning. But they have their miracles to hold on to and the worry is tempered by their deep faith that God will take care of their little boy.